The Border War

Also by Ryan Thorburn

Black 14

Lost Cowboys

Cowboy Up

Pearn and Associates, Inc.

Boulder 2005

Like us on Facebook

Grant,
Enjoy the book!

[signature]

The

Border

War

THE BRONZE BOOT RIVALRY BETWEEN COLORADO STATE AND
WYOMING

Ryan Thorburn & Robert Gagliardi

Burning Daylight

Colorado

Burning Daylight is an imprint of Pearn and Associates Inc.

Cover design by Paperwork. Photographs are provided as a courtesy of the Colorado State University Photo Service, the University of Wyoming Athletic Department and Eric Tippeconnic.

Library of Congress Catalog Number: 2018954260

Thorburn, Ryan & Gagliardi, Robert.

   The Border War.

ISBN 978-0-9897242-8-9

Printed in the United States of America

————————

The authors would like to thank Kevin McKinney, Diane Dodson and the rest of the University of Wyoming's athletic department, as well as Colorado State's Gary Ozzello and Paul Kirk, for their assistance with this project.

Contents

Foreword

By Kevin McKinney and Gary Ozzello

I'm not sure there is anything in sports better than a college football rivalry. Not only is each game a new adventure, but it fuels the fan base and usually produces memories that add to the tapestry that is each school's tradition.

The Border War has produced a corral-full of heroes, leaders and tons of legacy through its three centuries. There's been all kinds of good associated with the game, with a little bit of bad mixed in. Colorado State and Wyoming have enjoyed an extremely healthy and robust rivalry through the years with a tremendous amount of respect.

One thing is certain, it has been very special to a pair of states bordering each other. And, like any rivalry dripping with tradition, it's all about, "I remember when. . . ."

I saw my first Border War game in 1958 when my dad took me to Fort Collins at the stadium on College Avenue. Like Cowboys fans everywhere, my dad wasn't a CSU fan — no way, no how. And, he instilled that in me. Back then there were no gleaming stadiums, there was no concussion protocol. Those games were long on dirt, blood and guts — and short on flash.

The score escaped me until I looked it up (7-6), but I remember the Cowboys lost, and I remember crying about it on the way home. It hurt. Losses to arch rivals should.

My feelings for the Rams grew from there, and never wavered. If you are a Cowboys fan, that's just how it has to be. For me, Wyoming beating the Rams is as good as it gets.

While my blood boils a little bit — okay a lot — when I see CSU take the field, it doesn't diminish the fact that my best friend in the business has been working at CSU almost as long as I have been working at Wyoming. Between us we have a combined 95 years with the rivalry. When talking about writing this foreword, Gary Ozzello and I had a wonderful time reminiscing about the games and what made them special — the players, the coaches and the memories.

I've known Gary longer than anyone with whom I've been associated in this business of collegiate athletics. I respect him more than any, and I'm proud to call him my friend.

He's still a Ram, though, which I chose to let go long ago.

His memories are coming a little bit later, but for now we'll look at mine. I really enjoyed comparing notes with Gary on our favorite games. I imagine you wouldn't be shocked knowing that his favorite memories happened to be CSU victories, and mine involved Cowboys wins. His best memories were my worst. Of course, our experience spans 50 years of a centuries-old rivalry. We totally understand that there were many great games in this series years before we came along.

The CSU names that Gary mentioned were certainly familiar to me, and I'm sure to many Cowboys fans as well. Names like McCutcheon, Bell, Baker and Van Pelt. Greg Meyers, one of the greatest safeties to play in the old Western Athletic Conference. Running back Steve Bartalo, to this day, is one of the toughest backs I have ever seen. Do you remember Cecil Sapp and Kevin McDougal?

The Rams have always had big, tough linebackers, guys like Jeff Harper, who had 32 tackles against the Cowboys in 1982. There was Tippeconnic, Nichols and King. Who could forget the bookend defensive ends, Joey Porter and Clark Haggans. These are all great names in CSU lore.

While Gary may have seen most of the games a little differently, and we have our own heroes, there's one point on which we can both agree. With all the great names and all the great games, the rivalry has been defined by two men, arguably the two greatest coaches in their respective school's histories. Paul Roach and Sonny Lubick were two gentlemen-of-the-game who always rose above all the hype and hijinks of the Border War with a tremendous amount of grace and integrity. How these two men went about their business reflected what makes this rivalry great. They represented their institutions as well as any who have coached during the three centuries of this game. They were successful far beyond their institutions' expectations, and they always handled the game with class. They were the highlight of this rivalry to me.

I don't have to go very far down memory lane for one of my best memories. In fact, it was just last season (2017) in War Memorial Stadium in Laramie. I call it Josh's Border War. Hollywood couldn't have done better. It had all the ingredients: a great defensive game, the Rams on the verge of retaining the Bronze Boot traveling trophy and quarterback Josh Allen coming through with a masterful final drive to deny them. Who will ever forget Drew Van Maanen's remarkable catch on third down to keep the winning drive alive? Great game, great win, great memory.

The other memorable game of the 2000s for me featured Cowboys running back Alvester Alexander and great Cowboys defense. It was one of the most lopsided games in the rivalry's modern history. Alexander scored a school record five touchdowns, and the defense pitched a shutout in a 44-0 win in Laramie. Defensive end Josh Biezuns produced 3.5 sacks to lead that defense.

Without a doubt, my favorite game in the series came in 1996. It was Wyoming's version of "The Drive." Seldom when these two teams played that both were good. This was one of those times. The Cowboys, in fact, were nationally ranked, but found themselves trailing 24-13 entering the fourth quarter. They pulled to within five after scoring on a short field thanks to a Rams fumble with 11 minutes remaining.

Trailing by that margin with eight minutes remaining, the Wyoming offense took possession on its own 4-yard line. That's where quarterback Josh Wallwork went to work. With super receiver Marcus Harris as his primary target, Wallwork completed eight passes while driving his team the length of the field. Running back Marcus Brigham carried the final six yards for the go-ahead touchdown. It was a marvelously engineered 96-yard, 14-play drive that burned over six minutes off the clock. It was a thing of beauty. Safety Brian Lee sealed the win for the Pokes with a pass interception with just 1:28 remaining. What a game!

As a young guy my memories of the Border War — there wasn't a Bronze Boot yet — was Wyoming's domination of the series during the 1960s. Those were the Lloyd Eaton days. In his first four seasons as head coach (1962-1965), the Pokes outscored CSU 113-31.

But during that era there was a Rams memory and an incredible heartbreak for Wyoming. That, of course, was CSU's "bounce pass" victory of 1966. The Cowboys were ranked 10th in the country at the time with names like Egloff, Frazier, Kiick, Toscano, Dirks, Nels,

Washington, Huey, Aylward and House. But on that sunny afternoon in late October at CSU's College Avenue stadium, the Rams spoiled what would have been a perfect season for the Cowboys. It was my longest ride home from Fort Collins, ever.

Gary can elaborate on that one, it's too painful for me.

Let's get back to what makes me smile. Like the 1968 game. It wasn't necessarily memorable because the Cowboys won easily, 46-14. But what did make it memorable is the fact it was the first Bronze Boot game, the greatest rivalry prize in the country, and the addition that made the rivalry even more important — almost sacred. What an unbelievable part of the Border War tradition it has become. It is the most meaningful of all rivalry rewards, in my opinion.

One of the most famous games in the rivalry, the 1978 game, was made so not by the play on the field, but the shenanigans prior to the game. Gary can go a little more in-depth, but the Rams may have been a little too hyped for the game. They didn't show up for pregame warm-ups but came in their buses a few minutes before the toss of the coin and off-loaded on the east concourse of Hughes Stadium. They surrounded the captains who were on the field for the toss of the coin, and when push came to shove, a huge brawl ensued. The Rams were assessed a 15-yard penalty to begin the game. The Pokes went on to win in an upset, 13-3. The amazing part of the whole day to me was that no CSU player got hurt running down the stands in cleats!

For Wyoming, the late 1980s were highlighted by Roach and his high-octane offense (really good defense, too). The 1988 game was a great memory as the Cowboys won 48-14 at Fort Collins. The Pokes were ranked 10th in the country, and an ambush by the underdog Rams was highly possible, almost expected. But quarterback Randy Welniak took care of any possible upset with an amazing performance.

On that late October afternoon, the "Wizard of Ord" (Welniak is from Ord, Neb.) carried the ball 20 times for 109 yards and two touchdowns and completed 15 of 22 passes for 171 yards and another touchdown. Those numbers were part of a 531-yard total offense explosion.

Those are a few of the great memories I have of the Border War, a perspective admittedly through Brown and Gold eyes.

Clearly, Gary has a different view.

***

Though separated by just 65 miles, memories and perspectives on each side of the Border War are a world apart.

I have known my dear friend, colleague and mentor Kevin McKinney for 45 years. He, in fact, saved my life in the spring of 1975. As a raw freshman attending Colorado State University and working in the sports information office for Tim Simmons, I wore shorts and a polo shirt to a Friday Western Athletic Conference baseball doubleheader in Laramie. In May.

Midway through the first game the snow hit. Kevin saved me with sweat pants and a coat, and I remain eternally grateful for his friendship through the years. My brother.

But when it comes to the Border War – which I've witnessed for those same 45 years – our views couldn't be more different.

Take the 1978 game, famous (or infamous perhaps) for the pregame fight between the teams. Ever looking for a psychological edge, Rams coach Sark Arslanian had his team warm up at the practice fields outside Moby Arena, then bus to the game for the coin flip. And, the team came to the field through the CSU student section at Hughes Stadium.

In a show of solidarity, both teams walked out to the hash marks on the field. A pregame donnybrook ensued when hostile words became hostile actions. It would be more than fair to say both teams shared equally in the blame.

No Rams fan will ever forget the 1994 game. With an ESPN national television audience tuned into the Saturday night special, Wyoming seemed in control of the game against coach Sonny Lubick's team, which came into the game ranked among the top 15 teams nationally with a glowing 7-1 record.

In the third quarter, the Rams trailed 24-7 and lined up in punt formation. Lubick and special teams coach Brian Schneider called for a fake punt. Punter Matt McDougal's pass to Andre Strode led to a CSU touchdown as the Rams reeled off 28 consecutive points en route to a conference title — the program's first since 1955. Wyoming claimed an ineligible player downfield on the pass play. Sour grapes.

In 1986, CSU featured one of the most competitive players in school history, former walk-on running back turned All-American Steve Bartalo. Show him Brown & Gold and he'd show you the door. Bartalo loaded the Rams on his back for a 20-15 win at Hughes Stadium that year.

Harry S. Truman was the U.S. President in 1948, the last time CSU had played in a bowl game — until Earle Bruce arrived in Fort Collins. In 1990, Wyoming rolled into Hughes Stadium that year ranked 17th, and left on the wrong end of a 17-8 Rams win that spring-boarded the program into the postseason picture for the first time in five decades behind an inspired defensive effort.

And, anyone on either side will not forget the 1966 "bounce pass" game. Mike Lude would etch his name in college athletics as a premier administrator. On this day, as CSU's coach, he called the "bounce pass" play that pushed CSU to a 12-10 victory over the 10th-ranked Cowboys at Colorado Field — the last time the rivals met on College Avenue before the Rams moved into new digs at Hughes Stadium west of town.

Between Kevin and I we have collectively witnessed over 100 games — including 39 in our duties representing athletics. A century of memories, distinct yet meaningful.

Chief among those memories is the mutual respect shared by coaches, athletes, and staff throughout the years. While certain memories may fade, Border War tales have stood the test of time, and in fact, have grown with each passing year and each passing meeting on the field.

Names like Lubick, Hughes, Davis, Bruce, dot the CSU history books throughout the storied rivalry. It has been a rivalry that has taken its roots into the community as well.

For instance, arguably one of the most recognizable figures in CSU athletics history is Thurman "Fum" McGraw, the school's first-ever consensus All-American (twice) who later was a coach, school and athletics administrator at his alma mater. His wife, Brownie, another CSU alum, was an award-winning educator who has a local elementary school named in her honor.

Their sons, Dave and Mike did the unthinkable: They played football at Wyoming. And their sister, Debbie, joined them on the sidelines as a cheerleader.

There has also been plenty of hijinks through the years. Plenty of mascot stealing, taunting and teasing. And the year someone with Wyoming loyalties burned "Wyo" into the grass turf at Hughes

Stadium in the early 2000s, prompting the school to install artificial turf.

To the pleasure of CSU fans, it was comforting to know the culprit knew how to spell the three-letter acronym.

 **Kevin McKinney** graduated from the University of Wyoming in 1971 and has worked for the athletics department since 1972. He was the longtime sports information director, and currently is the senior associate athletics director for external operations. McKinney enters his 21st consecutive year in 2018 doing radio color commentary for Wyoming football games and has done radio color commentary for Wyoming men's basketball for the past 45 years.

 **Gary Ozzello** graduated from Colorado State University in 1978, was the sports information director at his alma mater from 1979-2007 and was also the senior associate athletics director for community relations. His current title with the school is executive director of community outreach and engagement.

Introduction

There are a handful of iconic rivalries in sports history — Ali-Frazier, Bears-Packers, Bird-Magic, Bjorg-McEnroe, Duke-North Carolina, Nicklaus-Palmer, Red Sox-Yankees, and so on.

Every corner of the college football map seems to have an indelible rivalry — Army-Navy, the Civil War (Oregon-Oregon State), the Holy War (BYU-Utah), the Iron Bowl (Alabama-Auburn), Michigan-Ohio State, the Red River Shootout (Oklahoma-Texas), the World's Largest Outdoor Cocktail Party (Georgia-Florida), USC-Notre Dame — that gets the blood boiling on both sides.

For those with a rooting interest or ties to the Colorado State-Wyoming series, which has been contested 109 times (108 according to Colorado State, but we'll get into that later) and in three different centuries, it's hard to beat the Border War — an annual gridiron battle for the Bronze Boot traveling trophy.

Alumni of the schools, fans of the programs and the coaches and players that have participated in the Border War understand the magnitude and the tradition of one of the best kept secrets in sports.

True Aggies and old Pokes know where the "A" is whitewashed on the foothills above Fort Collins and how to get to Vedauwoo.

They know about Arslanian and Armey, the Bounce Pass and Boom Boom, CAM the Ram and Cowboy Joe, Devaney and Eaton, Fantetti and Fum, Glick and Geldien, Hill and Hughes.

They know it's usually much safer to take I-25 / I-80 than Highway 287.

They know Joe (Tiller) and Joe (Glenn), Kiick and Kvamme, Larimer and Laramie, Mountain States and Mountain West, Novacek and New Mexico Bowls, Old Town and Prexy's Pasture.

They know both teams have a history of quieting the crowd with notable road wins.

They know Roach and Sonny, Tie Siding and Timnath, Unrein and Vomhof, the WAC and the War, xanthic color schemes, Yarborough and the zip codes (307, 970).

The Border War began in controversy, survived what legendary sports writer Larry Birleffi described as a "football victory-famine" at Wyoming during the early days of the sport, enjoyed a renaissance after World War II and has been contested for the bronzed combat boot of a Colorado State veteran for the last half-century.

Over the years, there have been pregame brawls, postgame brawls, mascot fights, mascot thefts and Watergate-level paranoia in both locker rooms.

"I remember there was a game when Pistol Pete and CAM the Ram got in a fight," said former Casper Star-Tribune sports editor Ron Gullberg. "Pistol Pete picked up CAM the Ram and body-slammed him, broke a rib. It was crazy."

After Colorado State (known as Colorado A&M during the era) won 21-20 in Laramie on October 16, 1948, en route to the program's first bowl game, a group of bold Rams fans tore down the goalposts in the last meeting between the rivals at Corbett Field. After Wyoming's 8-0 win in Fort Collins on October 1, 1949, on the way to the program's first bowl invitation, students from both schools poured onto Colorado Field, where a melee ensued as the Aggies tried to protect the goalposts while the Cowboys tried to return the favor and rip them out of the ground.

Colorado State historian John Hirn described the unofficial birth of the Border War in his book "Aggies to Rams" as follows:

This game proved to be A&M's only loss of the 1949 season and the beginning of the "Border War" that has continued between the two schools. The term "Border War" had not been coined yet, but after 1949, people saw the rivalry as more than just football.

During Wyoming football's "Golden Age" in the 1950s, the Cowboys started to get used to having their way with Colorado State on the field and also engaged in rivalry shenanigans off the field.

"When I was at Laramie High and competed in track meets down in Fort Collins, I noticed near (Colorado State's) football field was a little metal building where they kept some sheep that people at the college were doing studies on," said James "Lefty" Cole, who lettered for his hometown Cowboys from 1957-59.

"Some of us got the bright idea as freshmen not playing in the (1956) game, which was in Laramie that year, to go down and steal a ram. We thought we would be big heroes for a few hours. This pen the sheep were in was a good six-feet high and was surrounded by a chain-link fence. There were four of us, and since you could drink 3.2 beer when you were 18 down there, we were all pretty much liquored up.

"To get the ram out of there, three of us pushed up the wire, one guy would steady him, and the rest would go around and lower him down. Once we got the ram up, it got away from us and fell and hit the ground pretty hard. It knocked him out, and we were all pretty nervous. We put him in the trunk and headed back up Highway 287 for Laramie. About halfway there we could hear him rustle around. When we got to Laramie we thought, 'What the hell are we going to do with him?'

"My buddy's dad had a lumber yard and a fenced back yard, so we put him in there for the night. The next morning at about 10 a.m. or so, there were calls being made to the fraternities on campus from CSU about this stolen ram. Supposedly, this ram was a high-priced one where a lot of tests had been done on him. They said that if we told them where the ram was they would come pick him up and not press any charges. After we sobered up, we felt that was a pretty good deal, but that kind of stole our thunder. Nobody heard we stole the ram, and we weren't heroes or anything. The next day we found out the ram was recovered, was in good shape and everything was fine and dandy."

Even during the worst of times, when both sides of the rivalry are struggling to win games, the Border War can make or break a season.

After the Black 14 incident at Wyoming, the Pokes' powerhouse program went into a downward spiral. Lloyd Eaton, who had led the Cowboys to back-to-back 10-1 seasons and the Sugar Bowl before kicking the 14 black players off the team in 1969 for asking to protest Mormon Church policies before the home game with Brigham Young, only enjoyed one victory during his final season in 1970 — a 16-6 win at Colorado State.

"It was just a rite of passage to beat CSU," said John Griffin, one of the three players dismissed by Eaton that returned to play for the coach the next season. "We were always very successful at beating them and our attitude was we were going to top them every year. Of course, we beat them in Laramie in 1969 and we beat them at CSU in 1970."

Starting with the 1949 game, Wyoming had beaten Colorado State 21 times in 25 meetings. The Rams' only win in the series from 1956 to 1973 was in the infamous "Bounce Pass" game in 1966.

But on a wintry November day in 1974, Colorado State broke through with an 11-6 win. It was the first time in the seven-year history of the Bronze Boot that the traveling trophy stayed in Fort Collins.

"I played in that game at Hughes (Stadium). It was terrible weather, a snowstorm, and the field was ultimately completely covered in snow," recalled former Colorado State quarterback and athletic director Mark Driscoll. "In those days some poor guy tried to shovel the snow between plays just, so they could place the ball. My recollection was it hadn't been that cold, so it was muddy. The field didn't have a good crown, so Hughes never drained right. It was a mud bowl and it was a bad game.

"We were ahead 11-6, and at the end of the game one of the Wyoming running backs broke a long run down the west sideline and took it in for a touchdown, but the officials called him out of bounds. I have no idea how that official decided that, but I'm glad he did. Fritz Shurmur was Wyoming's coach and he went crazy on the sideline screaming that he was not out. We ended up stopping them and that's how we won the game."

Colorado State finished 4-6-1 in 1974, but the Border War gave fiery head coach Sark Arslanian some momentum entering his third season rebuilding the Rams program from the ashes. Shurmur, who had been 3-0 in the Border War before the devastating loss in 1974, was fired after a 2-9 finish and replaced by Fred Akers.

In 1975, the Rams — who had not won back-to-back Border Wars since 1951-52 and had not won in Laramie since a 14-13 victory in 1955 — stunned Wyoming again with a 3-0 victory at War Memorial Stadium.

"We were ahead three to nothing, there were like two seconds left in the half, and Wyoming had taken a timeout. They were going to kick a short field goal to tie the game at the end of the first half," said former St. Louis Rams general manager Charley Armey, who was Arslanian's top assistant at Colorado State.

"In those days the guy that was timing the end of the half could use a gun and shoot a blank to signal the end of the first half. And he was standing right behind Wyoming's kicker and they snapped the ball and he shot the gun and the kid missed the ball. So we went into the locker room ahead three to nothing and the game wound up three to nothing."

The Rams went on to finish 6-5 for the program's first winning seasons since 1966.

"Wyoming's kicker, a guy by the name of Joe Marion, is an all-conference kicker. As I recall, he was still a straight-on kicker, he was not soccer-style, but he was the best kicker in the league," Driscoll said of the breakthrough win in Laramie. "So, Wyoming scurries out, lines up and snaps the football. The clock is running, and as the ball is put down and Marion is running toward the ball to kick it, the referee is behind the play. And in those days, when the half was over they would shoot a gun. So, as Marion is approaching the ball to kick, the time runs out and the referee shoots the gun.

"Well, Marion hits about one inch of the ball and he missed it. This time Fred Akers went nuts. There's two games in a row where

CSU won in the 70s and it was kind of controversial."

The Cowboys finished 2-9 in Akers' first season but earned an invitation to the Fiesta Bowl in 1976, despite losing for the third consecutive season to Colorado State. In 1977, the Rams' 29-13 loss at Wyoming probably cost them a major bowl invitation after a 9-2-1 finish.

In 1978, the Border War reached a crescendo with "The Brawl" before kickoff at Hughes Stadium.

"I wasn't sure what to make of the rivalry, and then we came in through the student section and a fight erupted," said former Colorado State quarterback and head coach Steve Fairchild. "It was almost kind of unbelievable to watch it unfold. That was a good way to get introduced to the CSU-Wyoming rivalry."

Longtime Wyoming equipment manager Michael "Mad Dog" Aanonsen started a new tradition — sleeping in the visiting locker room at Hughes Stadium — prior to his first Border War game in Fort Collins in 1980.

"I heard a rumor that somebody was going to go into our locker room and tear up all of our gear and stuff like that. I thought, 'The hell with this,'" Aanonsen said.

"After we got our locker room set up Friday afternoon and everybody went back to the hotel, I stayed in the locker room and stayed the night in there. Everybody said I was nuts, and I did it on the spur of the moment. I used towels to sleep on the floor. At about 4:30 in the morning, somebody is jiggling at the door, the door opens, and these two guys come walking in and they are giggling and laughing. I sit up near a chalkboard near the middle of the locker room, I looked at them, they looked at me and they said, 'What are you doing in here?' I said, No, the question is what are you doing in here? I told them to get the hell out of there and they left."

Two decades later, after spending about 20 nights of his life guarding Wyoming's equipment in enemy territory, Aanonsen was told that he was not going to be allowed to crash in the bowels of the off-campus stadium anymore. Someone burned the letters "WYO" into the grass before the Border War, and Aanonsen was considered a person of interest given his proximity to the pregame prank crime.

"I didn't go out of the locker room when I stayed there," Aanonsen said. "I didn't go walk onto the field."

Fairchild led a last-minute touchdown drive to deliver Colorado State's 28-25 victory over Wyoming in 1980, which gave Arslanian five Border War wins in his eight full seasons leading the Rams.

"I think there were 48 seconds left and we took the ball 80 yards and threw a game-winning touchdown on what ended up being the last play of the game," said Fairchild, who capped the dramatic comeback with the decisive scoring strike to tight end Mike Camp with four seconds remaining.

"That was the one year Pat Dye was the head coach at Wyoming. I remember that being just a very good football game. They played well, we played well, and it was back and forth. We were just fortunate enough to go down and win it at the end."

Arslanian was fired midway through Colorado State's 0-12 season in 1981. Assistant Chester Caddas took over the final six games, including a 55-21 loss at Wyoming. Leon Fuller did his best to rebuild the Rams, highlighted by a 6-5 season with wins over Colorado and Wyoming in 1986.

But the Rams went 2-21 over Fuller's final two seasons in 1987 and 1988, which coincided with the Cowboys winning consecutive Western Athletic Conference championships under Paul Roach.

"It was nasty," Steve Bartalo, the bruising and record-setting running back for the Rams from 1983-86, said of the gladiatorial nature of the Border War during a 2016 interview with the Fort Collins Coloradoan. "I mean, people pulling at your body parts under the pretense they were trying to get a fumble, spitting in your face when you're facemask to facemask with them. It was to be expected, and I'm not saying it was one-sided either. It went both ways. It wasn't somewhere you wanted to take your young children and have them on the sidelines."

Rams fans carried the goalposts down to a local watering hole, CB&Potts, after Colorado State's victory in 1994 at Hughes Stadium. Pokes fans tore down the goalposts after Wyoming's 35-28 win in 2003, as Joe Glenn's team ended some of the frustration of Wyoming losing to Sonny Lubick's teams in the previous four meetings and eight of the previous 10 meetings.

"What I mostly remember about that is the Border War basketball game that winter in Laramie," said Kelly Lyell, a veteran sports writer at the Coloradoan. "Dale Layer was the CSU coach at the time, and they had like an 11-, 12-, maybe even a 13-point lead at halftime in Laramie, which was a big deal for CSU basketball. The Wyoming football team comes out at halftime. They bring out the boot, and Joe comes out and starts singing Ragtime Cowboy Joe. Then the fans get into it; the place went nuts.

"Wyoming's basketball team took that emotion and rode it to victory. I mean they just dominated the second half. It even carried over into another sport. I've never seen anything like that, something that didn't even have to do with anything in the actual basketball game, turn a game as quickly as that. It was pretty amazing."

What follows are more stories about the Colorado State-Wyoming rivalry from its bitter beginning in 1899 through the slippery snow bowl in 2017.

Whether you sing "Fight on, you stalwart Ram team" or belt out "He's a high fallutin', rootin' tootin' son of a gun from old Wyoming, Ragtime Cowboy Joe" on game days, or are just a fan of college football and all the pageantry that comes with it, the goal of this book is to enhance the appreciation for the Border War on both sides of the rivalry and nationally.

A Rivalry is Born — A look at the early years of
Colorado State vs. Wyoming (1899-1949)

Thirty-four years after the American Civil War ended, the football feud known as The Border War between Colorado State and Wyoming, two schools now separated by 65 miles of U.S. Highway 287, began on November 30, 1899.

Well, officially that's only a half-truth.

To this day, the sides disagree on the all-time series ledger. Entering the 2018 season, Colorado State's media guide shows the Rams leading 57-46-5, while the Cowboys say they actually trail their bitter rivals 46-58-5.

That's right, the team on the wrong end of the score in the first meeting recognizes the loss, and the winner doesn't count the game at all.

"You know Kevin (McKinney) and Tim (Harkins), they've never been able to count," former Colorado State sports information director Gary Ozzello says with a laugh, referencing his longtime Wyoming counterparts. "Kevin and I, we've been around a while, but we were not at that first game. As you go back and look at the records and the history, it gets fuzzy. . . .

"I think it adds to the lore of the series. Here are two rivals who can't even agree on how many times they've played."

Colorado Agricultural College (now Colorado State) opened

its doors in the fall of 1879, three years after Colorado became the
38th state, with a small enrollment on the Fort Collins campus. The
University of Wyoming was established in 1886, four years after
Wyoming became the 44th state, with 42 students and five faculty
members in Laramie.

The gridiron controversy dates back to the Thanksgiving Day
game on the high plains of Laramie at the end of the 19th century.
Colorado State made the trip north of the border to play Wyoming's
fledgling program for the first time on a shoddy field.

The Aggies had finished 3-5 against other in-state teams
during their inaugural season in 1893. After a 67-0 loss to Colorado
in Boulder on October 27, 1894, school president Alston Ellis banned
"foot-ball" at Colorado State. The sport returned to campus in 1899
with the hiring of the program's first head coach, W.J. Forbes, for $25.
The Aggies were drubbed at Colorado (63-0) and by Colorado Mines
(49-5), and then tied Northern Colorado (5-5) before their first road
trip out of state.

Wyoming's inaugural game was a 14-0 win over Cheyenne
High School on February 22, 1893. The Cowboys actually won their
first nine games from 1893-1897 against the likes of the Laramie
Town Team, Wilson Beauties and No. 5 Hose Company.

The visit from the Aggies was Wyoming's first game of the
1899 season.

According to the account of the game published on December
1, 1899, in the Laramie Republican, the crowd was unruly and the
two officials, one provided by each side, disagreed on the rules of
engagement. The Republican reported that E.D. McArthur, "the
Laramie druggist and an expert football player," was the umpire, while

Mr. Doane of Fort Collins was the referee. Colorado State historian John Hirn's research indicates that the Aggies' representative on the officiating crew was Edward House, a Colorado Agricultural College professor.

The Republican game story headline reads: 16 TO 12 — Colorado Agricultural College Team Defeated by University Boys. But the Fort Collins Express and the Collegian reported that House declared the Aggies 11-0 winners by forfeit after a disagreement with McArthur on the rules of play. The score listed in Wyoming's media guide is 12-0 in favor of the Aggies.

According to the Republican, as Colorado Agricultural College walked off the field, the Cowboys ran the ball in for a touchdown and declared themselves 16-12 winners of a violent contest that went into dispute with the Aggies leading 12-11:

"Fort Collins refused to play, but when the referee called on the sides to play, part of the Collins team lined up and Laramie, after waiting several minutes for the Collins men to line up, put the ball in play and made a touchdown, the score being 16 to 12 in favor of Laramie and the game ended, it being after sunset."

The Republican also mentioned the lack of crowd control and made the first public plea for help with the upgrading of Wyoming's athletic department facilities:

"The crowd persisted in getting on the field during the game and interfering very much. . . . The university must have a football grounds that are fenced in and have bleachers and a strong fence to keep the crowd off the gridiron. . . . Will some of Laramie's wealthy citizens take the lead and donate a handsome sum for grounds, which can be fenced off and used for athletic purposes? The football field

should have been gridiron with five-yard lines. As it was yesterday, only the 25, 40 and 55-yard lines were marked and made decisions more difficult than necessary."

As the mob of locals stormed the field after the incident, the Colorado Agriculture College quarterback was struck on the head by a cane. According to Hirn, school president Barton Aylesworth declared that Aggies would never play the Pokes in any athletic event until a written apology from Wyoming had been sent to him. When Ozzello and his staff revised the Colorado State media guide in 2009, it was decided that since the NCAA does not recognize forfeited games that were not completed, this original Border War, along with the Northern Colorado forfeit in 1900 and the Colorado forfeit in 1901, were struck from the athletic department's records.

"How do you take a rivalry over the top? You don't even agree on what the series record is," said Ron Gullberg, who covered some classic Border War games during his time as the sports editor of the Casper Star-Tribune. "That's wonderful. It adds some history and intrigue to the whole thing."

Despite the bad blood from the first meeting, Wyoming made the return trip to Fort Collins in 1900. Player-coach George E. Toomey led the Aggies to a 16-0 victory over counterpart William McMurray's Cowboys. The Aggies also won 17-0 in 1903 in Fort Collins before settling for a 6-6 tie in the 1904 meeting in Laramie. After an 0-6-1 start in the series, the Cowboys lassoed their first win, 10-0, on November 24, 1910, in Laramie, which was documented by the Republican:

"With ideal weather, a large crowd and abundant enthusiasm, the University of Wyoming yesterday afternoon defeated the Colorado Agricultural college at football ten to nothing, and did it easily,

gracefully, good-naturedly and enthusiastically, wading through the heavier line of Farmers and scoring three times. The game was replete with splendid features, the Cowboys showing how they are at last coming into their own, taking their places among the football players of the west and lining up for the future in a manner that brings enthusiasm to the front wherever they appear on the field. The boys have done some faithful work this year, and they are reaping the fruits thereof. They have been well trained and show their training, defeating two good teams in less than a week and coming out fresh as daises. . . .

"They are a gentlemanly lot of fellows, under the direction of Coach (George) Cassidy, a splendid, broad-shouldered athlete from the University of Vermont, and enjoyed their stay in Laramie. The Fort Collins aggregation will weigh an average of 13 pounds per man heavier than they Wyoming boys, but for all that they were not able to do much in the way of smashing through lines and carrying the doughty youngsters off their feet during the game."

Harry Hughes, Colorado State's longest-serving coach (1911-1941), posted a dominant 20-4-4 record against Wyoming. The Aggies won the Rocky Mountain Athletic Conference eight times (1915, 1916, 1919, 1920, 1925, 1927, 1933, 1934) under the direction of the "Dean of American Football Coaches." The 1925 team drubbed Wyoming, 40-0, to improve to 9-0 before a perfect season was spoiled with the travel-weary Aggies' 41-0 loss at Hawaii. Colorado State later honored Hughes, who also served as the school's athletic director until 1953, by naming Hughes Stadium (1968-2016) after him.

During the same era, John Corbett served as Wyoming's coach (1915-23) and athletic director (1915-39). Corbett posted a 15-44-3 overall record in eight seasons — Wyoming did not field a team in 1918 due to an influenza epidemic — including a 1-8-1 mark against the Aggies (the teams played twice in 1919 and 1920 with the Cowboys losing all four meetings).

On October 14, 1922, Wyoming suffered its most lopsided defeat in the history of the series with a humiliating 66-0 loss to the Aggies on homecoming in Laramie. The Cowboys finished 1-8 in 1922 and 0-8 in 1923, Corbett's final season as coach. After the Colorado State debacle in 1922 — Wyoming also lost 33-0 in Fort Collins in 1923 — the Laramie Boomerang noted that a bad football team can demoralize a university campus:

"It is true that athletics are of decidedly secondary importance to the scholastic possibilities and attainments of any college or university, but few students and but few alumni and far fewer prospective students become attached or remain loyally attached to a school whose athletic teams are continually at the bottom of the list."

In 1925, W.H. "Lone Star" Dietz coached Wyoming to its first winning record since 1911, when the Cowboys beat Colorado State in Hughes' first season to finish 4-3-1 (one of the wins was 74-0 over Laramie High). Dietz's 1925 squad finished 6-3, which included a 40-0 loss to the Aggies in the finale. After six more losing seasons over the next seven years, Willard "Dutch" Witte was hired to coach basketball and football. Witte's 1934 Wyoming basketball team was retroactively awarded the national championship by the Helms Foundation, and his 1935 football team capped the season with a 6-0 upset of future Heisman Trophy runner-up and U.S. Supreme Court Justice Byron "Whizzer" White and the Colorado Buffaloes. After the satisfying victory in Boulder, the Wyoming administration bused the team to the Savoy Hotel in Denver for a weekend celebration.

In 1938, Colorado State and Wyoming joined Brigham Young,

Colorado, Denver University, Utah and Utah State in the Mountain States Conference, also known as the Skyline Conference. The Buffaloes and Utes dominated the conference in football, combining to win or share nine of the first 10 championships. The Aggies and Cowboys played to scoreless ties in 1938 and 1940 as the ominous clouds of World War II were building on the horizon.

Wyoming coach Bernard "Bunny" Oakes, who was fired from the same position at Colorado after the 1939 season due to players revolting over his harsh style, lost 27-0 to Colorado State in 1941 and 10-0 in 1942. Wyoming, which won the 1943 NCAA championship in basketball, did not field a football team from 1943-46 due to the great war. After Hughes' final season in 1941, the Aggies were coached by Julius "Hans" Wagner, a standout player on the 1925 RMAC championship squad, during wartime. Colorado State did not field a team in 1943 or 1944.

The end if the war was an opportunity for growth for both universities and their football programs. Colorado State's enrollment increased from 1,023 in 1945 to 3,518 in 1946. The Aggies had 169 players to open practice in 1946, but after losing 33-0 at Denver and 47-0 at Utah State, Wagner was forced to resign, and Hughes returned to the sideline on an interim basis. The Aggies lost their final four games to finish 2-7. Hughes then hired Bob "The Whip" Davis, whose .618 winning percentage from 1947-55 remains the best in school history. The Aggie-Rams defeated Wyoming 21-6 in the 1947 game marred by 175 yards of penalties.

After cycling through 15 coaches and mustering only 13 winning seasons in the first 50 years of football, Wyoming president Dr. George "Duke" Humphrey changed the direction of the program dramatically with the hiring of athletic director Glenn "Red" Jacoby.

In 1947, Bowden Wyatt, an All-American for General Robert Neyland at Tennessee, was lured to Laramie by Jacoby to transform the Cowboys into a post-war powerhouse. Plans for a new football stadium were also in the works, and ground was broken on the $1.5 million stadium project for War Memorial Stadium on March 1, 1950.

Entering the 1949 season, Colorado State had a 30-5-5 record (29-5-5 not counting the 1899 game) against Wyoming. That includes a 21-20 victory on October 16, 1948, in front of a split crowd of 7,600 in Laramie. After Wyoming legend Eddie "Boom Boom" Talboom had a potential game-tying extra point blocked by Dale Dodrill, the Aggies fans in attendance tore down the goalposts on Corbett Field. Davis' squad capped an 8-2 regular season with a 29-25 win at Colorado, which led to an invitation to the Raisin Bowl on January 1, 1949. The Aggie-Rams lost 21-20 to Occidental College in Fresno, Calif., to spoil the Hollywood ending to the historic campaign for the "Cinderella Rams."

A half-century after the contentious first meeting, the Colorado State-Wyoming rivalry began to really heat up again on October 1, 1949, when the two teams met in Fort Collins with championship aspirations. Wyatt's Pokes opened the season with lopsided road wins at Idaho State (58-13) and New Mexico (41-14), while Davis' Aggie-Rams escaped with road wins at Colorado College (14-7) and Denver (14-13). The student governments of the schools created a cowboy boot trophy for the game, but this original traveling trophy never became a tradition, according to Hirn's research.

According to documents from the Mountain States Conference in Wyoming's archives, the Cowboys were the highest scoring team in the country in 1949 at 37.5 points per game. The numbers were inflated by a 103-0 victory over Northern Colorado (known as Colorado State

Teachers College at that time). The Bears vowed to never play the Pokes again following the blowout for the ages. The two programs have only met one time since the infamous game, a 35-7 Wyoming win in 2013. The 1949 game remains an NCAA record for most points scored in a game, along with the 15 touchdowns and 13 extra points. The Cowboys outscored their opponents 375-65 that season.

"All those days of sweat, blood and tears on the practice field began to pay off in the season of 1949," J. Douglas Reeves, a three-time letter-winner for Wyatt (1949-51), wrote in a collection of alumni manuscripts published by the University of Wyoming in 1965.

"Those bone-crushing nights in the old armory in February and March, the six weeks of spring practice outside in April and May, and Sunday practices in the fall began to show up in the total team ability. The regimentation of the training table (even for married players), controlled diets and the constant demands for above average physical stamina, all played a part in the climb to the top."

The Aggies, led by Thurman "Fum" McGraw and Dodrill, were ready for a defensive slugfest. Wyoming defensive tackle Charles Peterson recorded a safety in the fourth quarter to break a scoreless tie, and Walker "Sonny" Jones scored a touchdown run on a reverse to cap the Cowboys' 8-0 victory in front of an overflow crowd of 12,500 at Colorado Field. Fans of both teams scrambled onto the field after the game to either protect or tear down the goalposts. A riot broke out, and teargas was used to separate the fighting students.

"Wyoming's 8-0 win over Colorado State's Aggies in a night game at Fort Collins will always rank as one of the toughest games in which I ever took part. It ended with a squabble among the fans and the famous tear-gas incident," Reeves recalled. "The year before, in Wyoming's 21-20 loss on Corbett Field that was climaxed by one of the biggest free-for-alls in Wyoming's history; so, 1949 was not much different at Fort Collins, but we won."

For the Aggies, the bitter defeat turned out to be the only loss of the season. Colorado State's seven-game winning streak after the Border War concluded with a 14-7 win at Colorado. The Cowboys' victory was the first of six consecutive shutouts for Wyoming, which also led the country in the lowest pass percentage by opponents that season.

Both teams finished the 1949 season with 9-1 records. Wyoming's lone loss came in the second-to-last game of the season — 32-7 at Baylor. The Cowboys won the conference title with a 5-0 mark. Neither team went to a bowl game. Colorado State's players voted not to play against Arizona State in the Salad Bowl scheduled for January 2, 1950, in Phoenix. Xavier University made the trip instead and defeated the Sun Devils, 33-21. Wyoming also received and declined a bowl invitation after negotiations with the Grape Bowl in Lodi, California, broke down. The Cowboys were not guaranteed enough money to pay for all 50 players to make the trip.

The 1949 Border War signaled a shifting of the guard in the rivalry as Wyoming won 21 of 25 meetings.

Rise of the Cowboys — The golden age of Wyoming football (1950-69)

The golden age of Wyoming football began with the opening of War Memorial Stadium for the historic 1950 season. The Cowboys christened the 17,500-seat venue with a 61-13 romp over Montana State on September 16, 1950. Fortunately for the Bobcats, the scoreboard was not finished in time for the opener. A crowd of 17,268 showed up a week later for the official dedication of the stadium. Baylor, which handed the Cowboys their only loss in 1949 (32-7 in Waco, Texas), made the return trip to Laramie. Wyoming shut out the nationally-ranked Bears, 7-0. Royal McMullen scored the lone touchdown running in place of an injured Eddie "Boom Boom" Talboom, who still managed to kick the extra point. Baylor quarterback Hayden Fry, who went on to have a hall of fame coaching career at Iowa, drove the visitors down to the Wyoming 3-yard line and the 1-foot line, but Wyoming's defense stuffed the Bears with two goal-line stands to preserve the win.

Colorado State (Colorado A&M during this era) was the homecoming opponent on October 7. A record crowd of 19,565 watched Talboom rush for three touchdowns and pass for another during the Cowboys' 34-0 romp. The Aggies had entered the game on a nine-game winning streak dating back to their previous defeat, the contentious 8-0 home loss to the Pokes in 1949. Bowden Wyatt's emerging powerhouse finished the 1950 season 10-0, the program's first undefeated season (not counting the early years where it played only a handful of games) and ranked No. 12 in the final Associated Press poll. Wyoming outscored its opponents, 363-59, including four shutouts and three games where the Pokes allowed only seven points.

The Cowboys also accepted an invitation to play in their first bowl game — the Gator Bowl.

"This year's team has done more than anything in history to unify our state and its people," proclaimed university board of trustees president Milward Simpson, a three-sport legend at Wyoming who captained the 1920 football team and went on to become the state's governor and a U.S. Senator.

"Someone will have to prove to me that this team can be beat. I won't believe it until someone does."

The Cowboys, who made the trip to Jacksonville, Florida, by train, dominated Washington & Lee, 20-7, in the New Year's Day game.

"Football practice was no joke," J. Douglas Reeves recalled in a memoir about his Wyoming playing days. "Coach Bob Woodruff of Florida, who was helping our coaching staff, said it was rougher than his spring practice. We practiced twice a day for two weeks, then held a scrimmage on the second Saturday that was better than the Gator Bowl game. Coach Wyatt admitted to me later that we came along so fast in Florida, and were so ready to play after that scrimmage, that he was afraid we would lose a little edge before the game, which was still a few days away. . . .

"Offensively, Eddie Talboom used the same procedure and plays that had worked so well all season. Before halftime that old feeling was there that we could chalk up the first-ever bowl game victory for Wyoming."

Wyatt wasn't quite able to recapture the magic of the 1950 season as the team finished 7-2-1 in 1951 and 5-4 in 1952. In his final two seasons at Wyoming, Wyatt lost to Bob Davis' Aggies — 14-7 in 1951 and 14-10 in 1952. Wyatt, who was inducted into the College Football Hall of Fame as a player in 1972 and as a coach in 1997, left Laramie to take the Arkansas job.

Wyoming went 10-0 in 1956 under Phil Dickens, finishing 19th in the final AP poll but without a bowl appearance. The Pokes had defeated Texas Tech in the Sun Bowl after the 1955 season and were hoping for an invitation to the Gator or Sugar Bowl, but none came. The perfect season included a 20-12 win over the Aggie-Rams, who finished 2-7-1 in Don "Tuffy" Mullison's first year as head coach. The victory in Fort Collins started a 10-game Border War winning streak for Wyoming. Dickens left for Indiana University after the 1956 season and was replaced by Bob Devaney, who went 5-0 against Colorado State. Wyoming's road to the Sun Bowl in 1958 included a 7-6 victory over the Rams in Fort Collins.

"The 1958 game is the one I remember the most," said Jim Walden, nicknamed the "Mississippi Gambler," whose 29-yard touchdown pass to Bob Sawyer in the third quarter delivered the comeback win for the Pokes after Mike McGill added the extra point. "Number one, it was a horrible game played by us and them — 7-6 is not that overpowering. If you look at the papers, I don't know how much they wrote about it, but we didn't dress everybody in those days. All of our scout team guys, our redshirts and transfers, didn't dress. We only took a 50-man squad and played one-platoon football. But all of the football players would still come down to Fort Collins because it was only 60 miles away, best I remember, so they would all come down there and get about half-tanked. What else would you do in those days besides raise hell and get drunk?

"When we get off the field, I'll never forget this, we came out of the dressing room and are made aware that there are cops everywhere. The sirens are going off and there are fights all over the place. We get on the bus and start to drive out. Coach Devaney is sitting up on the right front seat, I'm about three rows back, and he says, 'Damn, that looks like some of our guys.' Some of us on the bus knew exactly who they were. There had to be 50 guys out there with Wyoming letterman jackets and they were fighting everybody.

"About half a dozen of them got thrown in jail. Coach Devaney had to go back down there and get them out of there. It was the damnedest thing. I always laugh and say, 'I don't know how the rivalry was on the field, but it was intense off the field.'"

The Border War finally heated up on the field in 1966 when Wyoming finished 10-1, including a 28-20 victory over Florida State in the Sun Bowl, but suffered its lone defeat to the Rams in the "Bounce Pass" game.

A year later, Wyoming fielded perhaps the best team in program history. The 1967 Pokes pounded Arizona (36-17) on the road in the season opener and Air Force (37-10) in the home opener leading into a rematch. The Rams nearly derailed Wyoming's perfect regular season and path to the Sugar Bowl.

Wyoming led 10-0 in the first quarter, but Colorado State cut the lead to 10-7 at halftime. All-American kicker Jerry DePoyster kicked a 55-yard field goal with 1:34 left in the third quarter to give the Cowboys their final points and a 13-7 lead. DePoyster missed a 51-yard field goal on Wyoming's next possession, and a 62-yard run by Larry Jackson set up a 33-yard field goal to cut Wyoming's lead to 13-10 with 8:21 to play.

Defensive back Alton Lavan intercepted a pass by Wyoming quarterback Paul Toscano. Lavan also was the Rams' kicker, but he missed a 46-yard field goal.

Colorado State had two more chances to tie or take the lead, but its own mistakes got in the way. The Rams executed a fake punt but were flagged for illegal procedure. On a Wyoming punt, Lavan was called for roughing the punter. The Cowboys ran out the clock from there.

That was one of three games for Wyoming during the regular season that was decided by three points or less. The Cowboys went into the Sugar Bowl against LSU ranked No. 7 in the country. Despite a 20-13 loss in the high-profile bowl game, they finished the season No. 6 in the final poll, and led the country for the second consecutive year in rushing defense at 42.3 yards per game.

Colorado State finished the 1967 season 4-5-1.

"I believe we were the better team while I was there, but Colorado State always got up for us and we played some intense games with them," Toscano said.

The glory years of Wyoming football were from 1949-69. The Cowboys were 151-51-9 over that time and finished .500 or better every season. Their worst records were 4-3-3 in 1957, Devaney's first season, and 5-5 in 1962, Lloyd Eaton's first season.

Wyoming has had 51 players earn All-America honors from 1949 to the present. Thirty-one of them played between 1949-69.

Talboom was Wyoming's first All-American in 1950. He still ranks sixth in NCAA history in career scoring average at 10.8 points per game from 1948-50. Talboom scored 303 points over 28 games, including 34 touchdowns and 99 extra points.

Thirty-two of Wyoming's 82 players who have been drafted by NFL teams played during that era.

Running back Jim Kiick starred with Larry Csonka in the Miami Dolphins backfield in the 1970s. Gene Huey played one year with the San Diego Chargers but went on to be a long-time NFL assistant coach. Dale Memmelaar played offensive and defensive line for Wyoming but was an offensive lineman for five NFL teams from 1959-67.

That era also featured some of the most successful coaches in school history.

Wyatt went 39-17-1 from 1947-52 and won two Mountain States Conference titles. He also started the "coaching carousal" pattern all too familiar for Wyoming and its fans over the years — coaches who had success in Laramie and then moved on to bigger jobs. Wyatt left Wyoming for Arkansas, where he was he head coach for two seasons. After that he was the head coach at Tennessee from 1955-62, was the Southeastern Conference Coach of the Year in 1956, and he led the Volunteers to the 1956 Sugar Bowl. The Kingston, Tennessee, native was also the athletic director for Tennessee from 1962-63.

Dickens, who also played at Tennessee, was the head coach at Wofford prior to being hired at Wyoming. Dickens went 29-11-1 in four seasons, including the school's second 10-0 season and a Skyline Conference championship in his last season in 1956. Despite not playing in a bowl, that team finished 19th in the final AP poll. Dickens left Wyoming for the Big Ten job in Bloomington, Indiana, but proved that the grass isn't always greener at bigger school. Dickens was investigated for recruiting violations with the Hoosiers. He was not allowed to participate in any coaching related activities during the 1957 season, and the NCAA placed the school on probation from 1960-63.

Wyoming hired Devaney, a Michigan State assistant, to continue the program's rise. Devaney's winning percentage of 75 percent (35-10-1) from 1957-61 remains the best in school history. His last four Wyoming teams were a combined 31-7-2 and won four conference titles. The 1958 team played in the school's second bowl game, and defeated Hardin-Simmons 14-6 in the Sun Bowl. The 1959 team finished 9-1 and 16th in the final AP poll, but didn't play in a bowl game.

"Bob Devaney was just an unbelievable competitor," said Walden, who lettered from 1958-59, leading the Cowboys to back-to-back Skyline Conference championships and earning conference player of the year honors as a senior in 1959. "He was one of the most pleasant people in the world on a day-to-day basis, but you knew he also was one of the most competitive, and he didn't stand for a lot of nonsense.

"You could tell a joke to the team, but then if you weren't practicing the way you were supposed to he would take your skin off. You just had to know that he was a wonderful human being and he cared about us, yet you were almost afraid of him in some ways because you didn't want to disappoint him. I was also afraid of him because I didn't want him to get on my ass. He could do it, boy."

Devaney went on to Nebraska where he went 101-20-2 from 1962-72, won back-to-back national championships in 1970-71 and eight Big 8 Conference titles. Devaney also served as Nebraska's athletic director from 1967-93. Walden, who went on the become the head coach at Iowa State and Washington State, was a graduate assistant coach at Nebraska for Devaney from 1969-70, and a full-time assistant from 1971-72.

Wyoming promoted Eaton, who had joined the staff as the defensive line coach in 1957, to replace Devaney. Eaton won 63 percent of his games (57-33-2), and his 57 victories from 1962-1970 is still a school record. The Cowboys were ranked for 14 weeks during the regular season under Eaton. They also played in back-to-back bowl games for the first time in school history in the 1966-67 seasons and won three consecutive WAC championships from 1966-68.

The 1967 season was arguably the best in school history. The Cowboys were ranked in the top 10 for the second half of the season, finished the regular season 10-0, but fell short against LSU in the Sugar Bowl, 20-13. The Cowboys finished the season ranked No. 6 in the country — their highest ranking in school history — due in large part to a dominating defense that held eight of its opponents to 13 points or less.

Despite a 6-4 record in 1968, Wyoming was ranked in the top 20 for three weeks. It started 1969 with six consecutive wins, but the run of dominance ended with what is known as the Black 14 incident. Eaton booted the 14 African-American players off the team prior to the October 18 home game against Brigham Young University because they approached him about protesting policies of The Church of Jesus Christ of Latter-day Saints they viewed as racist. The 14 players wanted to wear black arm bands during the game but were dismissed after a short, one-sided meeting with Eaton. Wyoming defeated BYU and San Jose State the following week at home but lost their final four games — all on the road.

The Cowboys did not have another winning season until 1976.

After Eaton left Wyoming, he was the director of player personnel for the Green Bay Packers for four years in the 1970s but was demoted to a scouting position after that. He later served as the western regional director for the BLESTO player rating service of the NFL, before retiring in the mid-1980s. Eaton died on March 14, 2007, at the age of 88.

Wyoming dominated the rivalry with Colorado State from 1949-69 with a 17-4 record. The Cowboys won 10 consecutive Border War meetings from 1956-65, the longest winning streak for any team in series history.

In 1970, the year after the Black 14 incident, Wyoming won only one game, but it was against Colorado State, 16-6, on the road. It was the third year the Bronze Boot traveling trophy was part of the rivalry.

"It didn't make a difference if it was Colorado State on that day, or Air Force, Colorado or New Mexico. We wanted to go out and beat somebody," said Conrad Dobler, who lettered as an offensive and defensive lineman for Wyoming from 1969-71 and never lost to Colorado State with the Cowboys.

Dobler went on to play in the NFL as an offensive linemen with the St. Louis Cardinals, Buffalo Bills and New Orleans Saints.

"It was a good rivalry. I played offensive line and defensive line against them. At that time the program was trying to rebuild itself," Dobler said.

"Everyone thinks you're the patsy on their schedule and a guaranteed win. I'm sure Colorado State thought about that. We straightened them out and let them know what the game was all about.

"We didn't like them. They didn't like us. They didn't like us going down to Fort Collins, drinking their 3.2 beer and stealing their women. They'd tell us we didn't have any women up there (in Laramie) they'd want to steal."

When asked what it felt like to keep the Bronze Boot the entire time he was at Wyoming, Dobler said: "It didn't mean a damn thing to us."

That would soon change.

Sonny Days in Fort Collins — Colorado State dominates series under Sonny Lubick (1993-2007)

Years before getting his first taste of the Border War, Louis "Sonny" Lubick parked cars at historic Naranche Stadium in his hometown of Butte, Mont., during the annual Montana-Montana State games. Lubick grew up in the middle of the "Brawl of the Wild" rivalry, which began in 1897, two years before the bizarre first meeting between Colorado State and Wyoming.

"The Bobcat-Grizzly game was something," Lubick recalled. "What I mean by that is it was the one thing that divided the entire state or brought the entire state together. It was the biggest sporting event in the state."

Lubick was an assistant at Montana State from 1970-77 and the program's head coach from 1978-81, a stint that included a Big Sky Conference championship and a 2-2 record versus Montana.

"That was a tremendous rivalry. Of course, sometimes as coaches you don't understand its impact or significance until you're in the middle of it or look back on it," Lubick said. "They started televising the game around the state when I was there, and then all the rural towns got the game, and that made it even more significant.

"That was your job-saving saving game."

Or job-losing game.

After the Bobcats' 3-7 finish in 1981, which included a 27-17 loss to the Grizzlies, Lubick was fired. He resurfaced in Fort Collins as Leon Fuller's offensive coordinator for three seasons at Colorado State. Fuller was Wyoming's defensive coordinator in 1976 before following Fred Akers to Texas. The Rams were coming off a dreadful 0-12 season in 1981, which included a 55-21 defeat to Wyoming in Laramie.

"Coming here in '82 with Leon and our staff, we were just trying to resurrect Colorado State," Lubick said.

Following a 28-14 defeat at Missouri, the program's 14th consecutive loss, Fuller notched his first win at Wyoming's expense — Colorado State's 9-3 Border War breakthrough in Fort Collins.

"I was (coaching) on offense then, and we were putting in a new passing game," Lubick said. "We hit a pass to Jeff Raikes, a Denver kid, for the only touchdown of the game. Leon's defense held Wyoming down."

Even though Fuller had spent a successful year with the Cowboys, who played in the Fiesta Bowl after the 1976 season, Lubick said the rivalry wasn't very heated in those days, although a crowd of 27,652 showed up to watch the soggy defensive slugfest on September 11, 1982, at Hughes Stadium.

"Coming from the Bobcat-Grizzly game, that was the all-encompassing game in my world," Lubick said. "CSU and Wyoming were both teams that were .500 at best. It meant more to the fans. We were just trying to line up and make some first downs.

"The fans always fuel the fire. I started to get a little flavor of it."

Colorado State lost to the Cowboys in 1983 (42-17) and 1984

(43-34). Lubick left to pursue other opportunities, working as an assistant for Jack Elway at Stanford for three seasons before joining Dennis Erickson at Miami, but his time as a popular assistant with the Rams would pay dividends down the road.

Fuller had a breakthrough season in 1986, leading Colorado State to a 6-5 finish, highlighted by the Rams' first victory over Colorado since 1958 and a 24-20 win at Brigham Young University. Colorado State also beat the Cowboys, 20-15, only to lose three of its last four games to fall out of contention for the Western Athletic Conference title. Fuller was fired after back-to-back one-win seasons in 1987 (1-11) and 1988 (1-10), which included losses to Wyoming during the program's back-to-back WAC championship seasons under Paul Roach.

"They had some nice players in 1986 and they probably would have gone to a bowl game if they had not lost the last game at UTEP," said Tony Phifer, who covered the Rams for the Fort Collins Coloradoan during the era.

"Leon, because he had coached at Wyoming, had great knowledge of the series and what it meant to the people up in Wyoming. He won his first Border War in 1982, then Wyoming went on a run on him. That's why he was fired, because he couldn't beat Wyoming."

Wyoming had possession of the Bronze Boot for five out of six years from the end of the Fuller era through Earle Bruce's four years as head coach. Then the Border War took a dramatic turn in the other direction when Lubick was hired as head coach after winning two national championships as Miami's defensive coordinator.

"I remember Sonny's response during his introductory news

conference, which was held after Miami's New Year's Day bowl game, when he was asked how long before CSU would be competitive with CU," longtime Colorado State sports information director Gary Ozzello said. "He said, 'I'm not worried about that yet. I'm worried about being competitive with Wyoming and Air Force first.'"

During his 15 seasons as head coach, Lubick posted an 11-4 (.733) record against Wyoming and a 9-6 (.600) record against Air Force. The only Colorado State coach who enjoyed more wins in the Border War series was Harry Hughes, who went 20-4-4 against Wyoming from 1911-41.

"I think he was really good at getting his team to play big games," Kelly Lyell, the Colorado State beat reporter at the Coloradoan, said of Lubick's impressive ledger in the Border War.

"Coaches love to say the next game is the most important game and all that, and I'm sure Sonny subscribed to that as well. He wanted them to play well every game, of course. But I think he knew there was a little more on the line when you were playing Wyoming, if for no other reason that that's what your fans and your boosters talked about all year long."

During Lubick's first season as head coach, Colorado State got off to a 2-6 start before beating New Mexico and UTEP ahead of the regular-season finale in Laramie. Wyoming was 7-2 overall and in position for a WAC championship with a 6-1 conference record. The Rams ran roughshod over the Pokes, 41-21, at War Memorial Stadium. Colorado State, led by quarterback Anthoney Hill, racked up 556 yards of total offense during the dominant performance broadcast regionally by ABC.

"I don't know that it gets the credit it deserves," Steve

Fairchild, who was Lubick's quarterbacks coach from 1993-96 and offensive coordinator from 1997-2000, said of the impact reclaiming possession of the Bronze Boot in 1993 had on the program.

"Sonny's first year we were 2-6 at one point, and then we won our last three. Wyoming was going to a bowl, and we absolutely killed them. It was probably as impressive of a game as any team Sonny had. It doesn't get a lot of recognition, but we went up there and just hammered them, really embarrassed them. That game set the tone for Sonny's career."

Inside the visiting locker room that gray November Saturday in Laramie, the Rams had a sense the 1994 season was going to be special. After a 7-0 start, which included road wins at No. 22 BYU and No. 6 Arizona, Colorado State rose to No. 12 in the Associated Press poll and hosted No. 18 Utah. The Utes escaped with a 45-31 victory in the first-ever matchup between two ranked teams at Hughes Stadium.

Two weeks later, with the door to the WAC championship reopened with Utah getting upset by New Mexico earlier in the day, Rams fans decided to tear down the goalposts when No. 14 Colorado State bounced back with a dramatic 35-24 comeback win over Wyoming.

The Rams went on to claim the program's first conference title since 1955, finishing the regular season 10-1 before losing to No. 20 Michigan in the Holiday Bowl.

"I think that was very significant from the fact that I don't know if any of us, including the coach, believed we could win at a really high level," Lubick said. "But I could sense our system developing and the players starting to believe we could win. You could feel the belief system in the assistant coaches, too."

Adding intrigue to the Border War was the relationship between Lubick and counterpart Joe Tiller, who crossed paths as young assistants on the Montana State staff in 1970, which was Lubick's first season with the Bobcats and Tiller's sixth and final season coaching at his alma mater in Bozeman.

Tiller replaced Roach as Wyoming's head coach in 1991 and had a 2-0 record against Colorado State before Lubick was tabbed as the replacement for Bruce. After getting trounced by the Rams in 1993 and watching Colorado State fans tear down the goalposts after the memorable 1994 game, Tiller's Pokes exacted a measure of revenge in 1996 with a dramatic 25-24 comeback win in Fort Collins, which earned Wyoming a spot in the inaugural WAC championship game at the expense of the Border War rival.

"That game for me was bittersweet because I liked and respected Joe Tiller and it was obvious that was going to be his last Border War," Ozzello said. "One of the most special things for me, honestly, about the rivalry is the people on both sides."

Tiller left for Purdue after the Cowboys finished the 1996 season ranked 22nd in the AP poll with a 10-2 record but no bowl invitation. Lubick would post an 8-3 Border War record during the rest of his career opposite Wyoming head coaches Dana Dimel (1997-99), Vic Koenning (2000-02) and Joe Glenn (2003-08).

The Rams, despite early-season losses to Front Range rivals Colorado and Air Force, won the WAC championship in 1997. Included in the nine consecutive wins to end the campaign was a hard-fought 14-7 win at Wyoming. Lubick's teams went 5-2 in Laramie during his 15 seasons leading the Colorado State program.

"I think it was just the way he built his teams. We loved

playing on the road," said Kevin McDougal, the Rams' star running back from 1996-99. "It was just the attitude of the players we had. Most of the guys on the team were borderline guys to begin with. A lot of D-I schools didn't want us, and we were on that bubble. We were overachiever-type kids. The mentality and the mantra of the teams he put together was, 'Hey, we're just as good. Let's show them on the field. We're going to come to your house, and you're not safe.'"

On May 26, 1998, eight schools from the bloated 16-team WAC, including Colorado State and Wyoming, decided to split and form a new conference, which became the Mountain West Conference. While the Rams won or shared three of the first four MWC titles, the Cowboys struggled with a 5-23 conference record and three last-place finishes over the same span.

"I think that's one of the biggest things is Sonny could have left during that era and even before to chase bigger paychecks at bigger universities," said former Rams quarterback Bradlee Van Pelt (2001-03).

"He came from Miami, so he knew what it was like to play with the big dogs. But the way Sonny is, that's not what it's about. It's about the kids, the family, the community, the university. You take Sonny Lubick out of Colorado State and you might not even be in the Mountain West, you might still be in the WAC. You might be like San Jose State or something."

Colorado State went 3-1 in high-profile matchups with Colorado from 1999-2002, which made the "Rocky Mountain Showdown" in Denver the No. 1 rivalry in the hearts and minds of many Rams fans.

"As coaches we didn't think that," Lubick said. "Of course,

we think every game is important, and the veteran coaches knew Wyoming was still very important. If you lose that game, some of the other games don't matter. It just happened during that time we played some tough, close games with CU in those days and we were getting 75,000 people at Mile High. So, of course, people would think that's it.

"So, the rivalry did shift a little bit. And then you throw Air Force in there, we always talked about our three major rivalries. But for the length of the rivalry and as many times as we played, the Wyoming game still ranks up there."

Colorado was not on the schedule during Lubick's first two seasons at Colorado State, but he went a combined 4-0 against Air Force and Wyoming from 1993-94. In 1998, the Rams lost to all three rivals during a frustrating 8-4 finish. In 1999 and 2002, Colorado State swept all three Front Range foes and won MWC titles.

"I think they felt like they had taken a step up where they were competing with CU for state dominance," former Casper-Star Tribune sports editor Ron Gullberg said of Lubick's program. "That cycle when Wyoming was horrible, combined with their focus on the CU game, their attention kind of shifted. Wyoming didn't seem to matter as much."

Colorado State was 10-2 before finishing the 2002 season with a puzzling loss to UNLV and a loss to TCU in the Liberty Bowl. After winning six conference titles (three WAC, three MWC) in his first 10 seasons, Lubick's dominant program began to slide. The Rams finished 7-6, 4-7, 6-6 and 4-8 over the next four seasons. Wyoming ended a four-game losing streak to Colorado State with a 35-28 win in 2003 and blanked the Rams 24-0 in 2005 as Glenn attempted to breathe some new life into the series and the Cowboys.

"I thought Joe brought an amazing energy to the Wyoming program. Because of him, it really kind of amped up the Border War because he was willing to talk it up," said Mike Brohard, the Colorado State beat writer for the Loveland Reporter-Herald. "Sonny was a little bit more quiet, but Joe kind of made him talk about it a little more, just because Joe was so fired up about the rivalry. Joe brought an energy to the rivalry, to the state, and especially to that Border War game. It was important to him. They wanted to win that game, and that became really apparent."

Despite all of the success during the Lubick era — Colorado State had appeared in two bowl games from 1893-1992 and nine bowls from 1994-2005 — the living legend was on the hot seat entering the 2007 season. The emotional campaign began with a heartbreaking overtime loss to Colorado in Denver and a four-point loss at No. 10 California. Entering the regular-season finale against Wyoming on November 23, there was a lot of speculation by fans and in the media that it could be Lubick's last hurrah as the Rams' head coach.

Athletic director Paul Kowalczyk had already made the decision to give Lubick the boot, even if he won the Bronze Boot.

"We knew we were done," said Dan Hammerschmidt, who was Lubick's co-offensive coordinator in 2007. "Sonny told us on Wednesday that he was going to be done, so we played the game knowing he was stepping down. And we won the sucker. It was a good win for us. We played decent on offense."

Gartrell Johnson ran for two touchdowns and caught a touchdown pass to lead Colorado State to a 36-28 victory at Hughes Stadium. After Glenn shook his counterpart's hand on "Sonny Lubick Field," the Wyoming coach spilled the beans to reporters.

"I'm the reporter he first told it to. Tony Phifer was writing the game story, and one of the things I was there to do was, if indeed it was Sonny's last game, was a story on, 'What has he meant to CSU?'" Lyell said. "I'm like, 'Well, I better get Joe Glenn.' Joe knows him well, and we're literally walking off the field at Hughes Stadium and I asked Joe, 'There's a lot of people that think this might have been Sonny's last game . . .' He goes, 'Oh, it was.' I said, 'Excuse me?'

"He said, 'It was Sonny's last game, he told me beforehand they fired him.' Nobody else believed me. I go back up to the press box, I had to play my tape back for Tony Phifer and Mike Brohard. Nobody believed me that Joe had really said that. And I ended up writing the story. The end of the career of the most successful coach ever is announced by the head coach of the rival. That was stunning."

Brohard ran down to Wyoming's bus before it departed for Laramie to confirm Glenn's quote.

"Joe's sitting there with his wife, and I said, 'Joe, just to make sure, Sonny told you this?'" Brohard said. "And he said yes. That's kind of how we found out. It wasn't like he was trying to break news for us or anything. I think he honestly thought we all knew."

Lubick informed the players it was his final game in the postgame locker room, which silenced the roaring Bronze Boot celebration.

"It was a weird week," Hammerschmidt said. "When he came out and said he was done on Wednesday, we couldn't believe it. Things always happen in coaching, but we didn't think they were going to do anything to Sonny, just because he was Sonny, you know. That was a weird deal because we had heard that he had told Joe something, and it was just interesting.

"It made it nicer when we won the damn thing."

Kowalczyk and Colorado State didn't officially announce the decision until three days later.

"I didn't agree with the way Sonny got fired. An athletic director can do what he wants to do, but the backstory about how it kind of went about and how it was pitched to him, it wasn't the right way," Brohard said. "It was like Kowalczyk didn't really know who Sonny was. But to give Sonny that win, and for him to exit that way, was phenomenal."

The Rams' coaching staff and players could all be found at Lucky Joe's Sidewalk Saloon in Old Town Fort Collins that night toasting to the greatest coach in program history with the Bronze Boot.

"We were all at Lucky Joe's drinking out of that boot. Man, that was the nastiest thing I've ever done, drinking out of that boot. I think the whole place drank out of the boot that night," Hammerschmidt said. "It was cool. The players showed up. I mean, it was probably one of the only times you could drink with the players because you weren't coaching them anymore."

In the first 10 years after the Lubick era, the Rams have gone a combined 9-21 (.300) in their three rivalry games — 2-8 against Air Force, 3-7 against Colorado and 4-6 against Wyoming.

"Without Sonny, I don't know if Bradlee Van Pelt exists in the form he did," Van Pelt said. "For better or worse, I'm not saying I wouldn't have found success, but Sonny Lubick, at least from my perspective, was the architect of an amazing team and a small dynasty in a sense. Having everything against him and not really a lot of advantages, I think everything Sonny brought to the table was himself and the way he encouraged people and allowed them to play and believed in them. Sonny wasn't about himself."

A decade later, Lubick mostly remembers how hard his team played the day he secured his 108th and final win as Colorado State's head coach against the program's oldest nemesis.

"It's a good feeling," Lubick said of reclaiming possession of the Bronze Boot as one more parting gift for the Rams. "As a coach, the game is over, and you want to go out there and shake Joe's hand or whoever the coach is. I coached against a few guys at Wyoming, and they were all good people. But all of the sudden the gun goes off, and the seniors run over to get the boot. As a coach you're happy for them, but the real celebration comes when you get into the locker room. . . .

"Beating Wyoming down here my last game, as a staff we were all on the hot seat at that time. To see our team play that hard, which they did all year, was good to see."

Border Wars for the Ages — Classic games from the Bounce Pass to the Snow Bowl

October 29, 1966, at Colorado Field in Fort Collins —
Colorado State 12, Wyoming 10

Many of the classic games between these two rivals have nicknames. This one is known as the "Bounce Pass" game.

Wyoming entered the game at Colorado State ranked 10th in the country with a 6-0 record and had allowed just 36 total points. The Cowboys ended up leading the nation in fewest rushing yards allowed at 38.5 per game that season. The Rams were 3-2 but coming off consecutive road wins at Utah State and Air Force.

The Pokes, despite committing four turnovers (three interceptions, one lost fumble) and racking up 50 penalty yards, led 7-0 at halftime on a nine-yard scamper by quarterback Rick Egloff. All-America kicker Jerry DePoyster also missed two first-half field goals from 43 and 50 yards.

Colorado State took the second half kickoff and cut the deficit to 7-3 with a 33-yard field goal by Al Lavan, which was set up by a 45-yard run by Oscar Reed. Wyoming punted the ball back to the Rams late in the third quarter, which led to one of the most infamous plays in the history of the rivalry. Colorado State started at its own 15-yard line but drove to the Wyoming 30. On a fourth-and-16 play, quarterback Bobby Wolfe threw a lateral to wing back Larry Jackson. The ball hit the ground first and bounced into Jackson's hands. The Cowboys weren't sure what was going on and thought it may have been an incomplete pass. But it was a lateral, and Jackson threw a 36-yard touchdown pass to Tom Pack to give Colorado State a 9-7 lead. The extra point was blocked.

"My first emotion after it happened is that CSU would get a flag as (Jackson) was yelling and cussing at Bobby Wolfe for throwing the ball in the ground," said Tom Frazier, a Wyoming linebacker and captain on that 1966 team. "Then he turned around and took a couple of steps backward and threw the ball. We were like, 'What in the world is he doing?'

"Next thing you know, Tom Pack was alone in the end zone."

Paul Toscano was an all-conference quarterback for Wyoming in 1967 but played safety in 1966. He said Colorado State ran that play earlier in the game, but with no success. Frazier said the Rams talked to the officials before the game to let them know they planned to run a play like that during the game.

Colorado State coach Mike Lude discussed the Bounce Pass strategy — aka the "Cowboy Special," which the Rams had been working on for three weeks — during a 2015 interview with the Fort Collins Coloradoan.

"You have to tell the officials before the ballgame because they could easily miss that it's so close, you know, that it is not a backward pass. Well, it's a backward pass. And so, we told them," Lude recalled. "It's the third quarter, we get to the 35-yard line, it's third down. Wyoming's really good. That's the only game they lose that year . . . I tell Paul Lanham in the press box, our offensive backfield coach, I say, 'got to put it on.' (He replies) 'Good idea.' Bobby Wolfe, the quarterback, loses control of the ball and throws it away. Paul wants to punt. The rest of the coaches say, no, no. I say we're going to put it on again.

"I tell Paul, we may never get this 35-yard line again. We're going to do it. And he says Mike, 'You're the dumbest head coach in America.' We do it. The rest is history. Wyoming guys are jogging back to the line of scrimmage, (Jackson) lays it out there to Tom Pack."

One person who was livid with the play was Larry Birleffi, the longtime Wyoming newspaper columnist and radio voice of the Cowboys. In a story written by United Press International that ran in the Laramie Boomerang the day after the game, Birleffi was quoted:

"If the play was accidental and if coaches and officials are willing to admit it wasn't planned that way, it must go down as a real fluke. If it was planned, it was simply and clearly intentional grounding of the ball and circumvention of the rules, which the rules committee in college football went out to clear up some years ago when the soccer shift and feigning of injuries became popular. If the officials were forewarned before the game to watch for the play, then it becomes even a greater rock on the part of the officials. I have good friends at both schools, and I'm sure they will agree with me."

Lude said in the UPI's game story that his team was going to use the bounce pass play the week before the Wyoming game against Air Force. However, the Rams didn't use it as they beat the Falcons comfortably, 41-21.

"It took a lot of practice to teach Bob (Wolfe) how to throw the ball so it would bounce right and wouldn't go out of control,"

Lude said. "It worked perfectly, especially when Jackson shrugged his shoulders and nonchalantly picked up the ball."

The play counted, but the game wasn't over. Wyoming answered with a 22-yard field goal by DePoyster to take a 10-9 lead early in the fourth quarter. Later in the quarter, Wyoming forced a Colorado State punt, but Dick Speights fumbled, and the Rams' Fred Morgan recovered the ball at the Wyoming 44. Colorado State converted a fourth-and-11 play on a 15-yard pass from Wolfe to Jackson, and the Rams kicked a short field goal for a 12-10 lead with two minutes to play.

"This is where my second mistake was," Frazier said. "I went in untouched and dove at the ball and it went under me. If I would have been a little lower I would have probably blocked that field goal."

On the fourth play of Wyoming's next drive, Egloff was intercepted by William Kishman, and Colorado State ran out the clock for the victory.

That was Wyoming's only loss that season. The Cowboys still went on to win the Western Athletic Conference title. However, it was one of the team's poorest games as its points scored were a season low. Wyoming was out-gained in total yards 322-258 and had nine penalties for 75 yards.

"(The bounce pass) really didn't lose the game for us," Frazier said. "We were ahead and in the fourth quarter, and they punted to us. Offensively, we scored 10 points. That was unusual for us. We didn't play real well offensively. They got two field goals, and the second one they should have never had because we fumbled the ball.

"The bounce pass was a fluke, but it still should have ended 10-9 (in favor of) Wyoming had I blocked that field goal."

The week prior to the game, staffers from Sports Illustrated were in Laramie doing a story on the team.

"I think we got a little cocky, personally," Frazier said. "We should have been much more focused, but we weren't."

After the victory, Lude was carried off the field on the shoulder pads of his players. Colorado State received votes in the national polls for the next three weeks. However, the Rams split their final two games and finished the season 7-3.

— — —

October 28, 1978, at Hughes Stadium in Fort Collins —
Wyoming 13, Colorado State 3

This Border War is remembered more for what happened before the kickoff — "The Brawl" — than the game itself.

With the visiting Cowboys nearly completing pregame warmups, and the fans settled into their seats minutes before kickoff, there was no sign of the Rams.

Colorado State coach Sark Arslanian decided to make a dramatic entrance by having the team bus roll up to Hughes Stadium moments before the already-heated rivalry game.

"We picked the players up at the hotel and brought them by bus and didn't even show up for the warmup," recalled Charley Armey, who served as Arslanian's defensive coordinator (1973-75) and offensive coordinator (1977-78) during his stint as a Colorado

State assistant. "We did our warmups and everything at the hotel, then we showed up just before we were supposed to. I think we got a penalty for delay of game.

"We brought our players down through the fans to fire up the rivalry."

The Rams were coming off an impressive 9-2-1 season, which included a 29-13 loss at Wyoming. They entered the Border War with a bitterly disappointing 2-3 record. Arslanian, Armey and the staff were trying to shake things up with the unusual pregame routine, which included a stop on campus at Moby Gym, ahead of the intense rivalry game.

"The '77 team had been 9-2-1, and a lot of those guys were back in '78. We thought we were going to be pretty good," said Mark Driscoll, the former standout Colorado State quarterback from 1971-75 who was a young assistant on Arslanian's staff. "The team was kind of struggling. We weren't playing very well and we weren't living up to expectations. We talked in the staff meeting earlier in the week about, 'What are we going to do to get these guys fired up?'

"I still don't know whose idea it was, it was either Charley or Sark, but the idea was, 'OK, here's what we're going to do to get this team fired up. We're going to warm up back at Moby and we're going to drive out right before the game, we're not going to show up to the pregame warmup at all, and right before, at the appropriate time, national anthem or whatever it was, we're going to bring the team down through the stands on the student side. And if this doesn't get them fired up, nothing will."

About 10 minutes before kickoff, the Rams made their way down from the stands and circled the field.

"My experience that day is we had a bunch of high school recruits in for the game, Colorado guys, and I was the Colorado recruiter," Driscoll said. "I went out early and was kind of hanging out with the recruits. So, I didn't ride the bus and wasn't a part of that. What I heard was the guys were about to break the windows out of the bus they were so fired up sitting out there kind of waiting to come down."

Wyoming's players, led by captains Ken Fantetti (linebacker) and Marc Cousins (quarterback), were waiting anxiously at midfield for the coin toss.

"They started trash-talking us," Fantetti said. "There were twin brothers on the team, Mark and Mike Bell, and both played in the pros. They started giving me some crap saying they were going to kick our asses. Being the Wyoming Cowboy that I was, I said, bring it on! That wasn't a very smart thing to do since I was surrounded by 50 other people."

Mike Bell, a defensive tackle, was the No. 2 overall pick in the 1979 NFL draft who went on to play 13 seasons with the Kansas City Chiefs. Mark Bell was a defensive end and tight end who played six seasons in the NFL. The twin brothers, along with the rest of the Rams, were frothing at the mouth after a frenzied morning of last-minute preparation for the hated Pokes.

Colorado State held a team meeting only about an hour or so before the game back at the team hotel, which Mike Bell remembers being in the nearby town of Loveland, Colorado.

"So, Charley Armey gets in front of the whole team and says, 'Men, we're going to play a rivalry today that is a nasty rivalry. I'm going to put on some film today and you're going to see what I'm

talking about. And I'll tell you right now, if any of this happens . . .'
Mike Bell said.

"He got fired up the more he talked, and he turned on this film.
It was clips they put together, obviously of the worst possible cheap
shots throughout the years between Wyoming and Colorado State.

"I think they had a perfect angle of a CSU player who gets hit
late out of bounds, and Charley Armey starts escalating his voice and
says, 'I'll tell you right now, if this happens today, I'm going to be the
first one out there to kick his ass.'

"I'm telling you what, Charley had us so fired up. I remember
as a young guy, I couldn't even hardly see straight. I wanted to go kill
somebody. He had us so jacked up, all of us. He said the offense gets
on this bus and the defense gets on that bus. We were throwing chairs.
We were so hyped. We just wanted to play the game, but we had to
take the bus from Loveland to Fort Collins."

By the time the Rams arrived at Hughes Stadium, both teams
were on edge. Fantetti, a second-round pick who played seven seasons
with the Detroit Lions, said one of the Bell brothers threw the first
punch — at him — and the fight was on.

"It was an all-out brawl," Fantetti said. "There were fights
everywhere. By the time it was going good there were about 40 or 50
cops with batons and sticks trying to break everything up."

Mike Bell said Fantetti's memory of the incident is a little
fuzzy.

"I never threw a punch at nobody. My brother, who is an
identical twin, had words with him. At the coin flip he might have said,
'I'm going to kick your ass,'" Mike Bell said. "I don't know if there

were ever any punches thrown. There was a lot of shoving, guys going on the ground tackling each other, and I saw it getting kind of serious. I think Fantetti was part of it. Once they saw us walking down out of the student section, their team came out there and it didn't take much.

"It got serious. It got to the point where I realized we've got to stop this or it's going to be ugly. We got it calmed down."

According to an account in the Rocky Mountain Collegian, Colorado State's student newspaper, Wyoming center Greg Chytka threw the first punch, but Driscoll remembers the Rams' starting quarterback, Keith Lee, engaging Fantetti.

"Everybody was all fired up, jumping around, and Keith Lee just pushed Ken Fantetti," Driscoll said. "So obviously when that happened, there's the fight. Both teams emptied the bench and there was a big fight before the game even started."

Here's Fantetti's most vivid moment from the fight: "We had a freshman linebacker out there in the brawl, and CSU had five of their guys, including their starting quarterback, grabbing him. Four guys had him stretched out on the ground holding him down, and their starting quarterback was hitting in him in the face. I went over there and slammed the quarterback. I got a sack before the game even started."

Gary Ozzello, the longtime Colorado State sports information director, had a bird's eye view of the infamous Border War incident from the press box.

"The entire CSU squad was out at the hashmark. Then Wyoming did the same, their whole team came out to the hashmark. Then all hell broke loose," Ozzello said. "There were fights from one 10-yard line to the next. It's a donnybrook."

The Cowboys and Rams made national headlines before kickoff.

"The next day, I told (Wyoming SID) Kevin (McKinney), 'We made the front page of the L.A. Times,'" Ozzello said. "That game, Wyoming and Colorado State, prompted the rule now where there's a limit by the NCAA on how many people can be at midfield for pregame coin toss."

It took about 15 to 20 minutes to break up the fight, and according to the official game statistics Colorado State received a penalty for unsportsmanlike conduct before the game started.

Once the teams were separated, the Rams jumped out to a 3-0 first-quarter lead. Wyoming scored all of its points in the second and third quarters. The two teams combined for 21 penalties (12 for CSU, nine for Wyoming).

"They had a heck of a linebacker that year at Wyoming," Armey said of Fantetti, who was the WAC defensive player of the year in 1978 and also earned All-American honors. "The two teams met at midfield and before the game we had a little donnybrook right in the middle of the field.

"And it was my last game I ever coached in college because after that game I was relieved as my duties as assistant head coach at Colorado State."

According to game accounts, Armey was extremely upset about a 15-yard personal foul call that went against Mike Bell and set up a Wyoming touchdown. After the game he reportedly followed referee Gene Wurtz up the tunnel and into the referee locker room, berating him along the way, and had to be restrained.

Three days later, Armey was asked to resign his position and did so. But he says it wasn't the result of a postgame altercation with a member of the officiating crew but because he was made the scapegoat for the pregame brawl.

"During the ballgame, right in front of our bench, our quarterback (Lee) threw an interception and as he was coming over right in front of our bench he got blindsided," Armey explained. "It was a legal block, but he landed three feet from the sideline. Then when the play was over, I stepped on the field to help him up, and the official threw the flag on me for coming on the field. . . .

"The reason that the president gave for relieving me of my duties was the fact that bringing the players down through the stands and everything, he thought we embarrassed the university. The talk of me bumping an official and arguing with an official is not true at all. They just wanted somebody to, I guess, show their frustration. Because we actually lost that game, too."

Driscoll was on the headset when the heated verbal altercation between Armey and Wurtz began after Lee was injured.

"I don't know if the wind got knocked out of Keith Lee or whatever, but he was down, and it was right by our sideline. Charley walks out there to check on him. Because he did that, the official said he's out of the game," Driscoll said. "I'm on the phone with Charley, so I heard it. Charley misunderstood it and said, 'What do you mean he's out of the game?' The referee meant that, 'Hey, you came out to help him, he's got to take a play off because he's an injured player. That's the rule.' Charley thought for some reason that he got thrown out and he was so frustrated because we played badly. He goes crazy, and unfortunately, it's Wyoming lore. It cost him his job.

"It was one of the saddest days of my life. At the end of the day, that pregame plan didn't work out. The Rammies didn't play well, we were struggling, we couldn't get anything done."

McKinney has worked for Wyoming since 1972. He was the sports information director from 1975-2007, and since then has been its associate athletics director for external operations. McKinney also has done color commentary on the radio for Wyoming football games since 1998.

McKinney and Ozzello both remember a play near the end of the game where calmer heads prevailed, and it involved Mike Bell.

"It was near our sideline and our guy was tackled. A player from our sideline started getting into it with a CSU player. Bell came over, grabbed his teammate and simply said, 'enough is enough,'" McKinney said. "I thought that was a class act on his part."

As is the case in rivalry games, there are different sides to a lot of stories.

Fantetti said during this game, "Wyoming running back Bobby Davis ran a sweep near the Colorado State sideline and an assistant coach reached out and close-lined him."

However, McKinney, Ozzello and John Hirn, athletic historian for Colorado State, didn't recall an incident like that happening.

One of the players for the Rams in that game was Wade Troxell, currently the mayor of Fort Collins. Troxell, the starting center, said on a play out of bounds he rolled on the Wyoming sideline and an assistant coach kicked him. Troxell said that assistant was Oval Jaynes, who was at Wyoming from 1978-80 and was the athletic director at Colorado State from 1986-91.

Wyoming ended up 5-7, and Colorado State finished 5-6. But the 1978 Border War — contested three decades after the 1949 melee between the two programs — remains one of the most memorable in the history of the rivalry.

"We were the boss that day," Fantetti said. "The game wasn't high scoring, but we whipped them."

— — —

November 3, 1990, at Hughes Stadium in Fort Collins —
Colorado State 17, Wyoming 8

The Cowboys rolled south across the state line with a perfect 9-0 record, ranked 19th in the Associated Press poll and confident they would be keeping the Bronze Boot for the fourth consecutive year. Paul Roach, who was 3-0 against Colorado State as Wyoming's head coach and seeking a third WAC championship in four years, reportedly guaranteed a Pokes' win on his weekly radio show.

Roach denied providing any pregame motivation, but the Rams still ran with the bulletin board material.

"What really fueled us is we got word, I didn't hear it myself, but we got word that Paul Roach had been interviewed on his radio show and said that CSU wasn't tough enough to beat Wyoming, and that if CSU ever beat him he would resign," said Eric Tippeconnic, a senior linebacker on the 1990 Rams. "I remember that was kind of our rallying point the entire week was, 'Who's toughest?' There were even shirts made, that were given to all the players only, that said, who is toughest now? And we wore those, especially after we won."

Colorado State had not been tough enough to play in a bowl game since the 1949 Raisin Bowl. The Rams went 3-10 against Wyoming in the 1950s, won only the Bounce Pass game in the 1960s and only had a combined 8-12 record against the Cowboys during the 1970s and 1980s when the program in Laramie was recovering from the fallout over the Black 14 incident.

Many of the Rams had been recruited by Leon Fuller, who compiled a 22-55 record (.313) during seven seasons as head coach, including a 1-11 finish in 1987 and a 1-10 finish in 1988. Earle Bruce, the former Ohio State coach and Woody Hayes disciple, molded a group that was tired of losing into a team on the edge of a historic breakthrough season. Colorado State was only 5-3 overall, but 4-0 in Hughes Stadium entering the Border War.

"Definitely it was night and day when Earle Bruce came to town," Tippeconnic said of the iconic coach. Bruce died on April 20, 2018, at the age of 87. "I remember two-a-days in the middle of August, back when they had two-a-days in pads, and between practices we had to dress up to walk down to the training table. We had to tuck our shirts in, we had to have button-down shirts on. We couldn't just show up in T-shirts and sweats and tennis shoes. So, Bruce was all about changing everything, and the image was one of the first things. He was a disciplinarian. It was his way or the highway. There was no questioning what was going to be done, that's just the way it was.

"It was an immediate change. It was the antithesis of how it was in previous years."

Colorado State's defensive line set the tone early by dominating the line of scrimmage. After a safety and a field goal, the Rams had an early 5-0 lead. A short touchdown run by Todd Yert made the score 11-0, but the two-point conversion failed.

Wyoming kicker Sean Fleming — the school's career leader in scoring (324 points), field goals (57) and extra points (153) — missed field goals of 26 and 37 yards in the second quarter. The Cowboys got back in the game to open the third quarter as linebacker Pete Gosar, one of three Gosar brothers from Pinedale, Wyoming, to play for the Pokes, intercepted a pass by quarterback Mike Gimenez and returned it 10 yards to the Rams' 39 yard-line. That led to Wyoming's lone score of the game — a 19-yard touchdown pass from quarterback Tom Corontzos to wide receiver Shawn Wiggins. The Cowboys made the two-point conversion to cut the lead to 11-8.

Fleming had a field goal blocked in the third quarter, but it didn't result in any Colorado State points. Early in the fourth quarter, Wyoming had the ball at the Colorado State 11 and running back Jay Daffer took a handoff up the middle for eight yards. However, Daffer fumbled on his way the end zone. The ball, which was stripped by senior safety Adolf Renaud, was recovered by junior cornerback Harlan Carroll.

Colorado State's Brian Copeland fumbled the ball back to Wyoming, and with 2:01 to play the Cowboys had the ball at their own 37. The first two plays were a sack and incompletion. Then on third-and-16, Tippeconnic intercepted a Corontzos pass and returned it 33 yards for the clinching touchdown.

"All the buzz was about Wyoming being undefeated, nationally ranked, (defensive end) Mitch Donahue was an All-American, they were going to come in there and kill us," Tippeconnic said. "No one was giving us a chance. We knew we were going to win. We couldn't wait, we were champing at the bit. I don't think I slept the night before.

"I remember knowing we were going to win. We didn't come out and portray that to the press, but we knew we were going to win. We were preparing to win from the first moment we got ready for them — this is how we're going to win, this is the game plan we're going to implement to win. There was never any question that we weren't going to win."

Renaud intercepted Corontzos on Wyoming's next possession to remove all doubt. It snowed in Fort Collins the night before the game, and Colorado State attempted only 15 passes. The Rams ran for 163 yards and held the Cowboys to just 29 rushing yards.

Wyoming, which was on the verge of playing its way into a New Year's Day Bowl before the Border War, didn't win another game, and capped its season with a 17-15 loss to California in the Copper Bowl. Roach, who was also Wyoming athletic director, didn't resign but retired from coaching after a memorable four-year run.

"Now I don't know if (Roach) said that or not about us not being tough enough. He denied it in the press room after," Tippeconnic said. "I was speaking about it to a reporter, and he walked by and said, 'I never said that.'

"So, I don't know, I didn't hear it myself. But I did repeat it. I was a young kid."

McKinney said Roach told him he did not say anything like that in the days prior to the game. McKinney also said Roach was furious about it.

The Rams finished their regular season 8-4 and earned the program's first bowl berth in 42 years, drawing Oregon in the Freedom

Bowl in Anaheim, Calif. After a 49-yard touchdown pass by Gimenez to Greg Primus with 12:21 remaining and a 52-yard touchdown run by Yert late in the fourth quarter, Colorado State had a 32-25 lead. Bill Musgrave, the Ducks' star quarterback, engineered a touchdown drive in the final minutes. Oregon head coach Rich Brooks opted to go for a two-point conversion to win the game instead of settling for a tie with the extra point. Selwyn Jones made a tackle just short of the goal line to preserve the Rams' 32-31 victory, which was the first bowl win in program history.

"They had a quarterback that was as good or better than any quarterback we played, including (BYU's) Ty Detmer, the Heisman Trophy winner that year. Musgrave was incredible," Tippeconnic said. "His pro career doesn't really bear that out, but this guy was sharp. He could drop a ball into a receiver's hands like he was placing it there. It was really difficult to get to him, and personally I was really stoked because I sacked him, and it was hard to do. He'd get rid of the ball quickly. . . .

"I just remember going into that game with so much confidence, same as the Wyoming game. We were going to win, not just to show up. Bruce was saying that all week."

The memorable 1990 run was the only winning season in Bruce's four years at Colorado State. He lost his next three Border Wars and was fired following the 1992 season after several of his players alleged that he verbally and physically assaulted them during practices. Bruce admitted to being "a pain in the ass" to some players but claimed no psychological or physical damage was done.

"I just remember feeling hurt," Tippeconnic said of his reaction to the firing of Bruce, who posted a 22-24-1 record at Colorado State. "I think one of the reasons they used for getting rid of him was that he grabbed a player's face mask and shook it. You're talking about a little guy. He can't hurt any of these college football players. He probably hurt somebody's ego. But that's the excuse used to get rid of him. I think it was probably decided before that they wanted to let him go, but it gave them the reason to let him go. I was upset, but in hindsight, after him you have Sonny Lubick coming in and completely changing the program forever, bringing it to its greatest heights."

Lubick, who inherited some outstanding players recruited and developed by Bruce and his staff, which included a young assistant named Urban Meyer, went on to coach the Rams to six conference titles and nine bowl games.

"I know when people consider Lubick they consider him separately from the people who came before him, but I don't. I think we set the tone in the Earle Bruce era by going to a bowl game for the first time in 42 years and then winning the bowl," Tippeconnic said. "I think people started noticing CSU after that, and certainly that helped with some of those initial recruits who helped out Lubick. Everybody benefits from someone's previous work, and while he deserves all of the credit for everything he did, of course, there were people who helped him in those early years that were part of the Earle Bruce recruitment.

"We started the change in 1990. I don't think it was a separate from what Lubick did at all. He's the greatest coach in terms of record in CSU's history and he did more than anybody else, but I think we helped to establish that."

— — —

November 5, 1994, at Hughes Stadium in Fort Collins —
Colorado State 35, Wyoming 24

Wyoming got off to a fast start, Lubick reached into his bag of tricks and the goalposts ended up at a local watering hole after this wild Border War.

The game proved to be one of the more disappointing losses for Wyoming in the series and one of the most beloved memories of Hughes Stadium for Rams fans in attendance.

Colorado State was ranked 14th in the polls. The game was a sellout and televised nationally. This Border War game drew the largest attendance — 35,524 — than any other game in series history.

But the Cowboys took the life out of the capacity crowd by storming ahead 24-7 with 5:19 left in the third quarter after a 13-yard touchdown pass from quarterback John Gustin to wide receiver Marcus Harris.

"We were kind of the team that came into the game ranked and were supposed to win the game," Lubick said. "Wyoming coach Joe Tiller and Wyoming came down and they had a running attack we couldn't stop and, man, they had complete control of the game."

The Cowboys were in control, until a controversial fake punt.

Colorado State's Matt McDougal was back to punt, but instead of kicking the ball he threw a 35-yard pass to defensive back Andre Strode for a first down at the Wyoming 32-yard line.

Tiller tried to get the attention of the officiating crew, believing that they should have flagged the Rams for having an ineligible man down field.

No flags were thrown.

"Wyoming had them on the ropes, and CSU ran the fake punt," Tony Phifer said. "The player who caught the pass was eligible, but another player on CSU's team didn't get the memo and was illegally down field. It was blatant on the game film. It was just this huge momentum swing."

The Rams scored a touchdown on the drive and then another touchdown after Brady Smith forced a fumble by Wyoming running back Ryan Christopherson. The Cowboys punted on their next two offensive series, and the Rams scored two more touchdowns.

"People think it was a great call," Lubick said of the fake punt. "but there was nothing else we could do. Luckily, Andre Strode caught the ball, and we went down and scored."

Wyoming got the ball back with 3:38 to play but lost the ball on downs.

"We had them, but after the fake punt the wheels came off and we lost all momentum," Kevin McKinney said.

Then things got scary.

Fans started lining up to storm the field with about five minutes to play. As the clocked ticked, the crowd inched closer and a premature attempt to rush the field was made with 1:04 still remaining on the clock.

"It was an ESPN game. Lee Corso got on me pretty good

about the students coming on the field," Lubick said. "And we had to stop the game."

There was only one tunnel where both teams could enter their locker rooms at Hughes Stadium. The security guards were unable to prevent thousands of people from getting on the field as players and members of the media tried to exit.

"Oh my God, I'm going to die," a Colorado State cheerleader screamed as she tried to make her way to the tunnel.

An event staff worker suffered a heart attack during the field storming. Fortunately, he lived, but a helicopter had to transport him out of the stadium because of all the people there after the game.

Colorado State went on to its first 10-win season in school history and its first-ever WAC championship. Wyoming won its last two games to finish 6-6.

"I think that was so important to them," Ron Gullberg said.

"Wyoming had been good, and that was a big turning point in the series for Colorado State."

Lubick won six conference championships and posted an 11-4 record in Border Wars while Wyoming struggled to find its footing after the Tiller era.

"For me, the fact that Wyoming was up 24-7 and CSU came storming back, after the game you had the feeling that was a magical year, unlike anything I'd seen," Ozzello said.

Steve Fairchild, an assistant on Lubick's staff in 1994, still remembers vividly his late-night commute home after the thrilling finish at Hughes Stadium.

"It was like an 8 o'clock start at Hughes and the crowd was raucous and we ended up winning," Fairchild said. "I remember them literally taking the goal posts and walking them down Elizabeth Street all the way past (C.B. & Pott's). I was driving home and the students had that goal post, they were taking it back to campus. I have a piece of it today. That was really something."

— — —

November 16, 1996, at Hughes Stadium in Fort Collins — Wyoming 25, Colorado State 24

This one is simply known as "The Drive." After a 28-24 loss at San Diego State the week before, Wyoming needed to win in Fort Collins to capture the Pacific Division title in the expanded 16-team WAC. Joe Tiller's Cowboys were ranked No. 23 in the country with a 9-1 record, but Colorado State had won four consecutive games and was 7-4 overall, including 6-1 in the WAC. The Rams had also never lost a game in November during the Sonny Lubick era.

The winner of this Border War would earn a spot in the inaugural WAC championship game in Las Vegas against No. 6 BYU. It is one of the few times in this long rivalry that both teams had a lot riding on the outcome.

"It's a fairly nasty rivalry," Wyoming center Rob Rathbun, one of eight Coloradans who started for the Cowboys in 1996 and one of 25 on the roster that season, told the Associated Press before the game. "I think, and this is the case with a lot of the Colorado guys at

Wyoming, we'd rather have a team that goes 1-10 with that win being against CSU than to be a team that goes 10-1 and have CSU beat us."

Wyoming's starting quarterback, Josh Wallwork, was concerned about the weather slowing down the Cowboys' prolific spread offense, which was led by Biletnikoff Award winner Marcus Harris.

"The first thing that pops into my head is that it snowed Thursday, Friday, and all the way up until the game on Saturday," Wallwork recalled. "Being from Hawaii and California, that was my biggest nightmare playing in those freezing-cold and snowy games. We were in our hotel in Fort Collins, and I remember waking up and looking outside my room and saw snow banked up against the building, and it was still snowing.

"I thought it wasn't going to be any fun. It stopped snowing at game time, but there were huge banks of snow around the field."

The conditions at kickoff: 21 degrees, windy with light snow.

The Cowboys led 13-0 at halftime, but the Rams scored 24 un-answered points in the third quarter. Wyoming's offense committed five turnovers (three fumbles and two interceptions) in the game.

Wyoming cornerback Lee Vaughn, an in-state product from Cheyenne, recovered a fumble deep in Colorado State territory that set up a two-yard touchdown run by running back Len Sexton to cut the lead to 24-19. The Rams' next drive stalled at about midfield, but a well-executed punt pinned the Pokes at their own four-yard line with 8:05 to remaining.

"Their quarterback was struggling, so we elected to punt," Lubick recalled. "If we make a first down at midfield and go down and score, the game is probably over. You know how that goes. But we downed the ball on the four-yard line. They had 96 yards to go march down field to beat us."

That's when Wallwork and Co. went to work on Wyoming's version of The Drive.

"You could just feel the momentum switch," Ron Gullberg said. "It was like watching those old 49ers teams in the 80s with (Joe) Montana just surgically tearing apart the opponent. There was nothing CSU could do."

Wallwork, who injured his knee earlier in the game and left for a couple of plays, was 6 of 8 for 68 yards on the drive and completed passes to four different receivers. The Cowboys faced third-and-one and fourth-and-one situations but gained first downs on runs by freshman running back Marques Brigham, a Colorado kid that Colorado State didn't get. Brigham scored the game-winning touchdown on a six-yard run.

"Marques had a worried look," Wallwork said of the call on the game-winning play. "I said don't worry about it (offensive lineman Steve) Scifres is going to make a hole for you. Run behind him and hold on to the ball."

The Drive was 14 plays, 96 yards and lasted 6 minutes, 17 seconds.

"It was kind of a blur," Colorado State running back Kevin McDougal said of having to watch helplessly from the sideline as the Pokes executed their methodical, rhythm offense. "They just kind of got rolling, and nothing could derail it."

Wyoming's two-point conversion attempt after Brigham's touchdown failed, which meant all Colorado State, which got the ball back with 1:48 to play, needed to steal the win was a field goal. But on the second play of the Rams' drive, Wyoming junior safety Brian Lee — another player from Colorado and the Cowboys' career interceptions leader — sealed the game with an interception of junior quarterback Moses Moreno.

"The Drive was a killer," said former Colorado State assistant Dan Hammerschmidt. "We had Calvin Branch, who still holds all those records for (receiving) touchdowns. On the offensive side, we were doing pretty good. I just remember Marcus Harris was such a stud. That was a tough one in 1996."

It did prove to be the final Border War win for Tiller. After Wyoming's heartbreaking overtime loss to BYU in the WAC championship game, Tiller left to become the new head coach at Purdue. Tiller, who led the Boilermakers to 10 bowls in 12 seasons, including a Rose Bowl, died on September 30, 2017, at his home in Buffalo, Wyoming, at the age of 74.

Tiller's 39 wins at Wyoming is tied for the second-most in school history.

"The game was bittersweet for me from a CSU perspective, but it also was bittersweet knowing that was the last time I would see Joe Tiller coach against CSU," Gary Ozzello said. "I really respected him as a coach and how he did things at Wyoming."

Despite a 10-2 record and being ranked No. 22 in the final AP poll, the Cowboys didn't play in a bowl game. Wyoming led the nation in passing offense that year with 359.2 yards per game. Colorado State also missed out on a bowl game for the first time in three seasons but bounced back with the historic 1997 season, during which the Rams won the WAC and 11 games.

"That '96 thing left kind of a bad taste in our mouth losing at home," Steve Fairchild said. "but I think it was a catalyst for what was probably Sonny's best team in 1997."

— — —

November 7, 1998 at Hughes Stadium in Fort Collins —
Wyoming 27, Colorado State 19

Nearly two years to the day after "The Drive," Wyoming returned to Fort Collins for another dramatic win, which is remembered as much for the "Fog Bowl" that enveloped Hughes Stadium as the 2017 game will be for the snow at War Memorial Stadium.

On a chilly night, the Cowboys were 7-1 and winners of six consecutive games. The Rams were 7-3.

Wyoming led 24-6 at halftime, but during the break a heavy fog rolled in, and by the time the second half started you could barely see from one side of the stadium to the other.

The Cowboys' first offensive play of the third quarter resulted in a sack, a fumble and a Colorado State touchdown. Wyoming went three-and-out on its next possession, and the Rams scored another touchdown to cut the lead to 24-19.

A field goal by Aaron Elling early in the fourth quarter provided the final points of the game. Colorado State missed a field goal in that quarter, and Wyoming secured the win with an interception by senior defensive back Greg Van Leer.

"That was probably one of my most memorable wins, ever, as a coach," said Dana Dimel, who coached Wyoming from 1997-99 and is now the head coach at UTEP. "Being on the field that night was great. It was such a cool football setting with it being a night game and the fog."

The win vaulted the Cowboys to a No. 25 national ranking. However, they lost their final two games and, despite an 8-3 record, didn't play in a bowl game.

Colorado State was 8-4, but also didn't play in a bowl game.

"The fog bowl was a big win for Wyoming," Ron Gullberg said. "I thought they had turned the corner, but it was just a weird era. For that one game, that was a huge win for Dimel. Wyoming, at the time you had to beat CSU and you had to beat BYU, and I think he was struggling to beat them both. To get that was big.

"But they never capitalized on it. They went on and had the loss at Tulsa that took them out of a bowl game."

The 1998 Border War was Dimel's lone win against the Rams in his three seasons, and Wyoming's last until 2003. In Dimel's first season in 1997, a crowd of 34,745 packed War Memorial Stadium in Laramie to watch Colorado State win, 14-7. That crowd remains the largest in Wyoming history, and is the largest to watch any sporting event in the state.

"I remember that fumble by (fullback) Mike Patolo just changed everything," Gullberg said of the Pokes' costly turnover in the red zone, one of the few scoring opportunities in the defensive battle. "The stadium was sold out, it was CSU, and both teams were good. You had Sonny Lubick getting the Rams rolling, and Wyoming was coming off the WAC championship game. You could just feel everything deflate with that fumble."

The loss in 1998 was one of four to Wyoming in 15 games for Lubick, who coached Colorado State from 1993-2007. Dimel said he saw the Rams legend at a coaches convention in New Orleans in the early 2000s and recalled something Lubick told him about the coaching battles against each other.

"He said, 'Dana, I knew when I saw you before a game and you hadn't shaved, you had your game face on, and I was terrified of that,'" Dimel said with a laugh.

— — —

November 1, 2003 at War Memorial Stadium in Laramie — Wyoming 35, Colorado State 28

Two weeks prior to this game, Wyoming defeated BYU, 13-10, for its third win in Joe Glenn's first season as head coach. It was the Cowboys' first win over the Cougars since 1999, and fans tore down the goal posts at War Memorial Stadium after the game.

The goal posts came down again after the Cowboys snapped a four-game losing streak to their Border War rivals.

"That had never happened to me as a coach," Glenn said of having goal posts torn down twice in one season. "I don't think anyone else would let that happen today."

It marked the first time since the WAC championship season

in 1988 that Wyoming defeated BYU and Colorado State in the same season. Those were the highest points during a 4-8 campaign for the Cowboys.

"When we played Wyoming in 2003, I remember warning all of the players, 'Don't expect this to be the Coronado Marriott in San Diego,'" former BYU star Brady Poppinga, who grew up in Evanston, Wyoming, told the Deseret News. "This is going to be roughing it. We're going to stay at a truck stop.'

"They were laughing at me. We get to Foster's Truck Stop, and guys are looking at me like, 'No way. We didn't think it would be this bad.' Some of the doors wouldn't even lock."

In the 2003 Border War, Wyoming trailed 21-7 in the second quarter before rallying to seize a 28-21 lead entering the fourth quarter. Colorado State tied the game, and the Cowboys' scored the game-winning touchdown on a 51-yard pass from quarterback Casey Bramlet, a native son from Wheatland, Wyoming, to wide receiver Malcom Floyd with 10:17 to play.

"The throw to Malcom was a deep go-route, and I threw it a little too far, but he reached out and got it and kept his feet long enough to get into the end zone," Bramlet said.

Bramlet's only two scholarship offers out of high school were from Wyoming and Colorado State. He had one grandmother go to Colorado State, and another to Wyoming. Bramlet finished the game 23 of 36 for 337 yards with two passing touchdowns and one rushing touchdown. He is Wyoming's career-leader in passing yards (9,684), attempts (1,378) and completions (767), and is second in touchdown passes (56).

Floyd ranks in the top 10 in school history in receiving yards

(2,411), catches (186) and touchdown receptions (14). Floyd signed with the San Diego Chargers (now the Los Angeles Chargers) as a free agent in 2004, and spent his entire career catching passes from Philip Rivers until retiring in 2015. Floyd caught 281 passes for 4,876 yards and 33 touchdowns with the Chargers.

Bramlet recalls another memorable moment from that game.

"It was a nice day when the game started, but once we got into the fourth quarter and (Colorado State) got the ball back after we took the lead, it started snowing," he said. "We all thought the weather would help us win that one."

Bradlee Van Pelt, who had dominated Wyoming in the 2001 and 2002 meetings and was best known for stirring up the Rams' rivalry with Colorado, lost a fumble at the Cowboys' two-yard line just before halftime that completely flipped the moment of the game.

"I remember it was kind of a shootout. My center, Mark Dreyer, had some torn tendons in his right hand, so he's wearing a club. That game he was snapping with his left," Van Pelt recalled. "I fumbled the center exchange, we bungled it at the one-yard line right before the half. There were a lot of these small instances where we just simply didn't execute. It's hard because for how much talent we had there were these small issues we didn't overcome. We shouldn't have been getting beat. We were just a superior team, in my opinion."

Van Pelt threw for 205 yards and a touchdown and ran for 156 yards and two touchdowns in his final Border War.

The Rams, who were 7-3 and in contention for the Mountain West title before the road trip to Laramie, finished 7-6 with a loss to Boston College in the San Francisco Bowl.

"It was a tough trip back," Van Pelt said of the somber bus ride to Fort Collins after the Pokes wrestled the Bronze Boot away from the defending Mountain West champions. "I remember some Wyoming fan saying things to me as I was leaving the stadium with my father. It didn't make me happy.

"Of course, I'm not a violent man, so I didn't do anything. But it's things like that that I remember — how enthusiastic they were and how disappointing and difficult it was for us and myself leaving that field."

— — —

November 22, 2008, at War Memorial Stadium in Laramie — Colorado State 31, Wyoming 20

One year after Sonny Lubick's final game as Colorado State's head coach, an emotional victory over the rival Cowboys in Fort Collins, Joe Glenn, another affable, well-liked head coach, found himself sitting squarely on the hot seat entering the 100th meeting between the two programs.

Speculation was swirling entering the game that Glenn — who had broken the news to reporters that Lubick was being fired after the Rams' win in 2007 at Hughes Stadium — would be coaching his final game at Wyoming.

"Our joke the following year, knowing it was Joe Glenn's last game at Wyoming, was that we should call Sonny to get a comment,"

Kelly Lyell said. "It was virtually the same thing. The next year Joe Glenn coaches the Border War and it was the last game of his career at Wyoming."

Entering the regular-season finale in Laramie, the Cowboys were 4-7, including a 13-7 win at Tennessee, but a dismal 1-6 in conference play. This followed the familiar script of the Glenn era: Wyoming consistently beat Power Five programs (Mississippi, UCLA, Virginia) but struggled to compete against the top teams in the Mountain West (1-5 vs. BYU, 1-5 vs. Utah, 1-3 vs. TCU).

"It's been a great six years, if you've been asking me about my time since I've been here," Glenn, who had led Northern Colorado to two Division II national titles and Montana to an FCS national title before taking on the challenge of rebuilding Wyoming, told reporters earlier in the week. "There's been some great wins and some great people and just high times for me in my life. To have played in a Division I bowl game and to have played at places the likes of Tennessee and Florida and Texas A&M and Ole Miss and some of these places, Virginia, has been really sensational.

"But I would have to place the people and the players that I've worked with and that I know around the state as probably the highlight of my past six years."

While Glenn's run at Wyoming was ending, counterpart Steve Fairchild was still enjoying a honeymoon period with the Rams, who were 5-6 and in need of a win at War Memorial Stadium to qualify for a bowl game in his first season as head coach. Lubick's former offensive coordinator agreed to return to the collegiate game take over for his mentor after spending seven seasons in the NFL with the St. Louis Rams and Buffalo Bills. Fairchild became the third Colorado State graduate to coach his alma mater, joining Julius "Hans" Wagner

(8-11-1 from 1942, 1945-46) and Don "Tuffy" Mullison (19-40-1 from 1956-61). Wagner, the captain of the Aggies' 1925 Rocky Mountain Athletic Conference championship team, went 2-0 against Wyoming during his brief coaching career. Mullison, who also coached wrestling, went 0-6 against the Pokes.

It looked like Wyoming was going to get the boot back for its embattled coach after taking a 14-3 lead after a halfback pass from Wynel Seldon to tight end Chris Sundberg for a touchdown and an interception return for a touchdown by Ward Dobbs. But Billy Farris rallied the Rams with three touchdown passes to Dion Morton. Colorado State was invited to the New Mexico Bowl, where running back Gartrell Johnson set an NCAA record for combined rushing and receiving yards in a bowl game with 375 in a win over Fresno State. Fairchild's 7-6 record was the best in school history for a first-year coach (Mike Bobo matched the record in 2015).

"It was neat," Fairchild said of capping his first season by collecting the Bronze Boot and the New Mexico Bowl trophy. "That was probably one of the highlights of being the head coach there was getting to a bowl game by having to go up and do it against them on the road. I think that was Joe Glenn's last game. We had to win a couple down the stretch. It was great to see it for the university and for those kids because they had worked so hard."

The morning after the Border War, Wyoming athletic director Tom Burman fired Glenn, who was 2-4 against Colorado State after coming up short in Lubick's farewell game and being on the wrong side of what turned out to be Fairchild's only win over the Cowboys as a head coach.

"I think Joe Glenn certainly had people energized about the rivalry. Even though he didn't win it very often, he had people pretty excited and making a big deal out of it," Lyell said. "That (2008 game) was a really big deal for that CSU team and for Steve Fairchild.

"Obviously, it didn't lead to bigger and better things like everybody at the time assumed it would. They followed that up with three straight 3-9 seasons, but that particular year it was a really big deal. The senior class, as Billy Ferris said at the time, they were just sick of losing. Somewhere part way into that season they realized it was their last hurrah and they found a little extra.

"That senior class kind of willed them to victory with their emotion and how important it was to them. They won a game that honestly not many of us thought they had a chance to win going in."

— — —

November 27, 2009, at Hughes Stadium in Fort Collins —
Wyoming 17, Colorado State 16

Dave Christensen embraced the importance of the Border War to Wyoming fans and needed a win over Colorado State in the regular-season finale to get the 5-6 Cowboys eligible for a bowl in his first season as the program's head coach.

The Rams were playing for pride at 3-8 and winless in the Mountain West but had won the previous five meetings with the Cowboys in Fort Collins. Four of Wyoming's victories prior to the game were by a combined 13 points.

Austyn Carta-Samuels, whose younger brother K.J. transferred from Washington to Colorado State prior to the 2018 season, was the Cowboys' starting quarterback. Early in the fourth quarter, the small but fiery true freshman scored on 49-yard touchdown run to give the Cowboys a 14-13 lead with 14:25 to play.

"We ran a couple of quarterback lead zones where the running back came up to block for me, and we called that play with the hopes of just getting a first down," said Carta-Samuels, now an assistant coach at Missouri. "I remember patiently sitting behind those guys and watched the blocks develop, and I was like, 'Oh my God, there's a gap.'

"Typically, for somebody as slow as I was that didn't happen, but when I saw the gap I hit it."

As Carta-Samuels was running down the sideline he stiff-armed a would-be tackler to the ground.

"At that point I knew it was an angle game, and I didn't typically win those. I was thinking of a way to position my body to use the defender — or my arm — as a shield to get a couple more yards," Carta-Samuels said. "The defender went up high to tackle me. Imagine it as someone trying to hug your shoulders. It really opened up his helmet, and I remember my left-hand sticking right in the middle of his face mask.

"I didn't grab the face mask. I got it with my palm and pushed him down to the ground. It kind of propelled me forward. It was by far the most successful stiff-arm of my career."

Colorado State safety Mychal Sisson chased Carta-Samuels down near the end zone, but Carta-Samuels said he "willed his way" past the goal line.

But that wasn't the knockout blow. The Rams reclaimed a 16-14 lead with 6:57 to play on a 23-yard field goal.

What happened next for Wyoming wasn't as dramatic as "The Drive" in 1996 but was equally as impressive.

Carta-Samuels converted a third-and-11 into a first down with a 14-yard run. On fourth-and-six from Wyoming's 47-yard line, Carta-Samuels completed a seven-yard pass to wide receiver Greg Bolling. A 20-yard run by running back Brandon Stewart set up the game-winning 33-yard field goal by true freshman walk-on Ian Watts with 1:27 to play.

"I am pretty much used to it by now, so that is a good thing," Watts, who had booted two other game-winning field goals earlier in the season, said after his Border War-winner. "The previous two were to win the game, but if I missed it would still be tied. If I missed this one, we would lose, so this was a lot more pressure, and I actually felt more nervous on this one than any other kick I've taken this year."

Colorado State got as far as midfield on its final possession, but linebacker Ghaali Muhammad intercepted Rams quarterback Jon Eastman to secure the victory.

"We had no fear," defensive lineman Mitch Unrein said of Wyoming's mindset on the final drive. "We knew we were going to stop them. Everyone just went out there and did their job and that's how we came out victorious."

Wyoming was out-gained 352-233 in total offense and ran 11 fewer plays than Colorado State.

Carta-Samuels was 13 of 21 for 137 yards. He ran for 87 yards on 14 carries but netted only 34 due largely to four quarterback sacks.

"I still remember all of those plays, but more than anything I remember the relationships with those guys and watching everyone celebrate," Carta-Samuels said. "I remember looking up behind our sideline and there were Wyoming fans all the way up in that section. A game like that was not a wine-and-cheese party. People were screaming and getting after it. It was really cool."

The Cowboys played in the New Mexico Bowl, their first bowl game since 2004, and defeated Fresno State 35-28 in double overtime.

That was the first of four consecutive wins for Wyoming over the Rams. In fact, Christensen became only the third coach in Wyoming history to defeat Colorado State in his first four years. The others were Bob Devaney and Lloyd Eaton.

"One of the only disappointing things in my career up there was not beating them five times in a row," said Christensen, who is now an assistant coach with Arizona State.

Christensen's second win over Colorado State was a 44-0 shutout in Laramie in 2010, the Cowboys' largest margin of victory in the rivalry. The Cowboys were 4-2 entering their home game with the Rams in 2013 but lost 52-22. It was Colorado State's largest margin of victory in the series since 1925.

"There might have been a little bit of (overlooking Colorado State). Our guys in the program at the time never lost to them," Christensen said. "Also, you know how difficult it is to win every single year.

"I remember the celebrations in the locker room afterwards. I think we did a good job of honoring our state and university with how we competed in those games."

Christensen said he would put the Wyoming-Colorado State rivalry up against any rivalry in college football today.

"You can't base it off the population of the two schools or the areas they are located. To those people it is every bit as important as Auburn-Alabama and rivalries like that," he said.

Christensen's 2009 staff at Wyoming included Dan Hammerschmidt, a former Colorado State player and longtime assistant at his alma mater, who found himself on the other side of the rivalry.

"I'll probably get shot for this being in the book, but I went up to coach at Wyoming in 2009, and Dave Christensen let me do the talk for the Border War of course before the game," Hammerschmidt said. "So, I drew up a big drawing on the game-plan board and flipped it over and showed them exactly where the boot would be. I drew that baby up and said, "Boys, it's going to be right here, so when we win this sucker go grab it.

"Sure enough, they darted over there."

The Cowboys reveled in their first win at Hughes Stadium in 11 years, parading the boot around the Rams' field and then singing "Ragtime Cowboy Joe" with a strong contingent of brown and gold-clad fans in the stands.

"It made me angry, but they earned it," Colorado State fullback Zac Pauga said. "That's their right as the winning team of the Border War."

In an effort to turn the Rams' fortunes around, Fairchild decided to bring Hammerschmidt back as a Colorado State assistant immediately after the Border War.

"It was an interesting deal. I was going out of the stadium, and before I was out of the parking lot, Fairchild called and offers me a job as a receivers coach to come back," Hammerschmidt said. "So, I didn't even get out of the parking lot. Coaching decisions? But it's my alma mater, so you gotta go back."

Wyoming beat Colorado State in 2010 and 2011, leading to Fairchild getting fired. Hammerschmidt, who had already enjoyed his share rivalry wins as an assistant to Sonny Lubick during the Rams' glory days, still cherishes his lone Border War win with the Cowboys.

"It was fun. We had a good year and we had a good staff at Wyoming that year," Hammerschmidt said. "It was definitely an interesting night. After all those years, I don't think I had lost too many to them, I was lucky enough to win a bunch of games when we were at CSU coaching, when Sonny was there we won a bunch of Border Wars. But when you get up there, you just get fired up for the game no matter what side you're on. I was like 'I'm still fired up for this thing and I'm on the wrong side.'

"It was a little bittersweet. To go down there and win the Border War and get into a bowl our first year at Wyoming was huge, but obviously I remember the CSU victories a lot better."

— — —

November 4, 2017, at War Memorial Stadium in Laramie —
Wyoming 16, Colorado State 13

In a matchup that featured two talented veteran quarterbacks, Wyoming's Josh Allen and Colorado State's Nick Stevens, this game will be remembered for the weather that arrived at Laramie's elevation of 7,220 feet.

Call it the "Snow Bowl."

Many of the more memorable and exciting Border Wars have taken place in Fort Collins. This one in Laramie was the most recent in the series but will be talked about for a long time due to some late-game dramatics — and the second-half snowstorm.

What started as light rain in the early portions of the game turned into snowfall with wet, heavy flakes. By halftime the field was completely covered, and the grounds crew did all they could to clear the line markers and goal lines.

"It was cold and kind of a drizzle in the first half. As soon as the teams went into the locker room at halftime, it just started. That rain turned to sleet, then snow, then heavy snow," said Kelly Lyell, who was in the press box at War Memorial Stadium covering the game for the Coloradoan. "By the time they started the second half they were already having to shovel the yard stripes. I think by the end of the game there were probably a good two-plus inches of snow on the field. It was big, puffy white flakes and a really intense game.

"Certainly, Colorado State was less geared for that type of

a game than Wyoming was. Colorado State's skill players were receivers and a quarterback who could chuck the ball. They didn't have the kind of ground game Wyoming did."

Colorado State's All-American wide receiver, Michael Gallup, did not have a pass thrown his way during the second half.

"It was really hard footing out there for both sides," Rams head coach Mike Bobo said. "I think it just turned into an inside running game for both teams."

The Rams led 10-6 at the intermission and were still ahead 10-9 entering the fourth quarter. Colorado State added a field goal, and on the Cowboys' next offensive possession Allen ran for 11 yards but fumbled the ball. He was ruled down initially, but after further review, it was a turnover. Defensive back Shun Johnson forced the fumble, and linebacker Max McDonald recovered it on the Wyoming 49-yard line.

As the officials were about to make their call, Colorado State players could be seen dancing and celebrating on the field. That angered Wyoming fullback and team captain Drew Van Maanen, a Colorado product who walked on and became a four-year starter.

"This is our home turf. This is where we go to battle. This is where we do our work. To see some other guys dance on our field, that lit a fire in me and sparked something in us," Van Maanen said. "We knew we were going shut them up with our play instead of our actions."

After Colorado State converted one first down, Bobo decided to go for it on fourth-and-six from the Wyoming 35. The Rams mustered only four yards on a run play as defensive end Carl Granderson and nose tackle Javaree Jackson swarmed under running back Rashaad Boddie short of the line to gain.

"Because it was fourth-and-six and we couldn't get any footing. We had two timeouts and a chance to stop them. We felt like we had the numbers in the box, and came up a half-a-yard short," Bobo said on the decision to leave his offense on the field instead of possibly pinning Allen and Co. deep with a punt.

With 7:09 to play, Wyoming took over on its own 31. On the first play, Allen threw a 17-yard pass to Van Maanen in the flat where he dove to catch the ball. Despite the soft layer of snow covering the field turf, Van Maanen suffered stingers in both of his arms and had to leave the game.

The Cowboys' final six plays were all runs, capped by a three-yard touchdown by sophomore running back Kellen Overstreet, who did not have a carry until the fourth quarter, to give them a 16-13 lead with 4:21 left. Wyoming forced a three-and-out and got the ball back with 2:38 to play. Colorado State used its last two timeouts, and the Cowboys had a third-and-one from their own 36.

Allen was Wyoming's leading rusher in the game, and the weather conditions weren't conducive to throwing. Everyone in the stadium, including those on the visiting sideline, knew the ball would be in Allen's hands.

It was, and Allen gained two yards and a first down. The Cowboys gained one more first down for good measure to secure the victory.

"The difference was the quarterback being able to run the ball," Bobo lamented.

The win made Wyoming bowl eligible for the second consecutive season, and it played in back-to-back bowl games in 2016-17 for the first time since 1987-88.

"With these conditions and the first time I actually played in the snow, this will be a game talked about here for a long time here," said Allen, who is from Firebaugh, California, near Fresno.

Both teams ended the season with seven regular-season victories. Wyoming won its first bowl game since 2009 in the Famous Idaho Potato Bowl over Central Michigan. Colorado State played in its fifth consecutive bowl but lost its fourth in a row to Marshall in the New Mexico Bowl. Allen was selected by the Buffalo Bills with the No. 7 pick in the first round of the 2018 NFL draft. Stevens signed with the Denver Broncos as an undrafted free agent.

"I think it was a great game in the fact that it was tight throughout, both teams were good, it was important for both teams at the time, and the weather really changed the game at halftime," Mike Brohard said. "You saw two quarterbacks, who both made their name throwing the ball around, really only throw one pass of significance each in the second half, just because of the weather and the snow coming down.

"Bobo said after the game he had never coached in a snowstorm before. So, it altered the way he coached. He watched how his players were reacting and what the footing was. That was one of the most interesting Border Wars I've seen just because of how the weather changed that game at halftime."

Wyoming head coach Craig Bohl said his team, which trains at 7,220 feet, should always be prepared for inclement weather conditions.

"We talked about weather in our pregame meal," Bohl said. "I was a young coach, and I once heard Woody Hayes, the old Ohio State coach, say that if you are going to play in the North Atlantic, then practice in the North Atlantic. If you are going to play in Wyoming, you have to train in Wyoming. That's one of the reasons we go outside and mix it up in all these elements.

"This was a classic football game. Hat's off to Colorado State, they played hard, and so did we."

After the game, the Pokes rushed to the northeast corner of the stadium and grabbed the Bronze Boot for a snowy celebration with the marching band still playing its frozen instruments.

"It's great being a Cowboy," said linebacker Logan Wilson, who grew up in Casper, Wyoming "I'm going to remember this game for the rest of my life."

This was the 50th meeting between the two rivals for the Bronze Boot. The Cowboys' dramatic comeback win gave them a 26-24 edge since the programs began playing for the trophy in 1968.

"I do think it will be a Border War that will be remembered because of the weather and the way Wyoming won it," Lyell said. "Josh Allen kind of won that game with his competitiveness. He ran a couple of quarterback keepers where he should have been stopped for a loss or no gain and he just kind of plowed his way through and got three, four yards to keep drives alive at the end of the game. He drove them down to get final points and got the first down to keep CSU from getting the ball back.

"I'm sure in Wyoming annals that will always go down as a big-time game. Plus, you had Josh Allen in his last year. He's probably going to go down as one of the greatest, if not the greatest, Wyoming quarterback of all time."

Border War photos

Photos courtesy of the University of Wyoming,
Colorado State University Photography and Eric Tippeconnic

Colorado Agricultural College hosts Wyoming on Nov. 27, 1913, in Fort Collins. The Aggies notched the most lopsided win in the history of the series with the Cowboys, 61-0.

An official looks in on a scrum at the goal line during the Colorado Agricultural College-Wyoming game in Fort Collins on Oct. 4, 1919. The Aggies won 14-0 en route to a Rocky Mountain Athletic Conference title under Harry Hughes.

Colorado Agricultural College and Wyoming battle to a 7-7 tie on Oct. 1, 1921, in Fort Collins.

The Aggies and Cowboys square off on Nov. 4, 1939, in Fort Collins. Colorado A&M shut out Wyoming, 22-0, at Colorado Field.

Eddie "Boom Boom" Talboom breaks through the line of scrimmage during Wyoming's 34-0 victory over the Aggies on Oct. 7, 1950, at War Memorial Stadium. The Cowboys capped their undefeated season with a 20-7 win over Washington & Lee in the Gator Bowl.

Paul Toscano (No. 10) helped lead Wyoming to a 13-10 victory over Colorado State on Sept. 30, 1967, at War Memorial Stadium. The Cowboys finished the regular season 10-0 before losing to LSU in the Sugar Bowl.

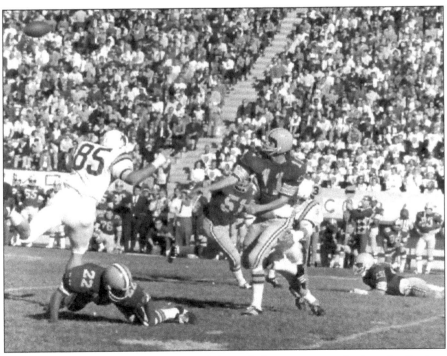

Colorado State quarterback Jerry Montiel throws a pass during the first Border War played at Hughes Stadium. The Rams, who lost 46-14 to Wyoming in the inaugural battle for the Bronze Boot, went 0-5 at home during their first season in the venue.

Two members of the Army ROTC guard over the Bronze Boot in the south end zone of War Memorial Stadium during Colorado State's 20-16 victory over Wyoming on Sept. 29, 1979.

Colorado State linebacker Eric Tippeconnic returns an interception for a touchdown to seal the Rams' 17-8 upset of No. 19 Wyoming on Nov. 3, 1990.

Three Wyoming tacklers take down a Colorado State ball carrier on Oct. 26. 1985, at Hughes Stadium. The Rams won the Border War that season, 30-19.

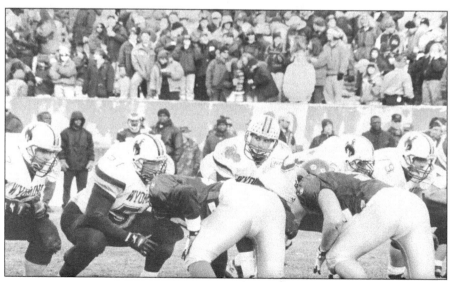

Quarterback Josh Wallwork (center) studies the line of scrimmage during Wyoming's dramatic 25-24 comeback victory over Colorado State on Nov. 16, 1996, at Hughes Stadium.

The Bronze Boot traveling trophy.

Cam the Ram takes the field with the Rams before the Border War on Nov. 7, 1998. Wyoming won 27-19 in foggy and muddy conditions at Hughes Stadium.

Colorado State quarterback Ryan Eslinger prepares to hand off to standout running back Kevin McDougal during the 1998 Border War. The Rams lost to Wyoming, 27-19, at Hughes Stadium.

Bradlee Van Pelt fights for some extra yards during his first start for Colorado State — a 42-14 victory over Wyoming on Sept. 29, 2001, at War Memorial Stadium.

Wyoming players celebrate with the Bronze Boot after defeating Colorado State 24-0 on Oct. 21, 2006, at War Memorial Stadium and 17-16 on Nov. 27, 2009, at Hughes Stadium.

Linebacker Brian Hendricks, whose father Mike and grandfather Joe played at Colorado State, comes up with a turnover for Wyoming during the Cowboys' 44-0 shutout of the Rams on Nov. 20, 2010, at War Memorial Stadium.

Wyoming quarterback Josh Allen with the Bronze Boot after the Cowboys defeated Colorado State 38-17 in their final appearance at Hughes Stadium on Oct. 1, 2016.

Images from the "Snow Bowl" game on Nov. 4, 2017, at War Memorial Stadium. Wyoming pulled off a 16-13 comeback victory to take a slim 26-24 lead in the Bronze Boot era of the Border War series.

History of the Bronze Boot Trophy

Two years after the infamous Bounce Pass game — Colorado State's controversial upset of 10th-ranked Wyoming, which spoiled a perfect season for the Pokes in 1966 — the Bronze Boot was introduced to the rivalry.

"There should be a hole in the toe to let the blood run out," Mike Lude, Colorado State's head coach from 1962-69, said when college football's newest traveling trophy was created.

Blood was literally shed inside the boot before it was bronzed.

The Bronze Boot is an actual size 8 jump boot worn by Captain Dan Romero during his service in the Vietnam War between 1966-67.

A half-century later, Romero's son, Jeff Romero, remembers vividly seeing his dad's combat boot inside his childhood home at 1604 South Whitcomb St. in Fort Collins, which is across the street from Colorado State's new on-campus stadium.

Unknown to Jeff Romero, his dad's right boot had already been prepared for mounting to a walnut base when he made the painful mistake of trying it on for size.

"It was in my parents' bedroom. I was like 4-years-old and I decided I wanted to put my foot inside my dad's boot," said Romero, a retired army captain and FBI special agent. "Well, it had a nail coming straight up through it, and I stepped on that nail. I had to get a tetanus shot."

Dan Romero grew up in Pueblo, Colorado, and played baseball and basketball at Adams State College before getting drafted into the army in 1960. He applied for officers candidate school in 1962 and served as an advisor to South Vietnamese units. While working on his master's degree at Colorado State, Romero and Major Vic Fernandez, who was also an assistant professor of military science at the university, came up with the idea for a traveling trophy for the Colorado State-Wyoming football combatants. Fernandez grew up in Trinidad, Colorado, and graduated from the United States Military Academy in West Point, New York. In 1968, Fernandez, a CSU Army ROTC cadre member, and Romero, a CSU Army ROTC graduate and cadre member, hatched their plan to honor Vietnam veterans and spice up the rivalry between the Rams and Cowboys.

"Two Southern Colorado guys found themselves at Colorado State and decided they wanted to produce a traveling trophy," Jeff Romero said. "They wanted a combat-worn boot, one that had seen action, so to speak. They picked one of my father's jump boots and they decided to bronze it. They came up with this whole idea of the Bronze Boot."

Following Romero's bloody mishap, his father's boot was bronzed. The scores of every game since the 1968 season are etched on the hardware. Through 50 Border War matchups with the Bronze Boot on the line, Wyoming held a 26-24 advantage, thanks to a comeback win in a memorable snow bowl in 2017 at War Memorial Stadium. The Cowboys ran to the sideline and grabbed the Bronze Boot after their 16-13 win in Laramie and will keep it in the program's specially-made trophy case until Colorado State's next win in the series.

"It was one of the most emotional games I've ever been a part of," Wyoming fullback Drew Van Maanen said of his senior Border

War experience. "The whole thing was just so emotional to me. I was just soaking everything in. And then when we finally got into that victory formation, we had talked all week that that's how we were going to end the game.

"Every one of us had confidence in that, and that's how the game was going to go, and then we did it. It was so surreal for me."

According to Colorado State athletic department historian John Hirn, following the 2005 season the original brass plate to record the winning games was moved to the back of the trophy to make way for a new plate on the front. The new plate has room for Border War scores through the year 2043, at which time a decision will have to be made as to how the scores will continue to be recorded on the trophy.

"It was always a rivalry. We didn't like going down there, and they didn't like coming up here," said longtime Wyoming sports information director Kevin McKinney. "But when the boot came along, it gave the game more meaning and validated that it was a rivalry. There's no question the rivalry became bigger for the kids because of the boot."

However, it took several decades for the Bronze Boot to be viewed as the prize possession it is for the two programs today.

"There was not a whole lot of fanfare," Jeff Romero said. "It was basically the two ROTC departments trading it off."

Wyoming had reeled off 10 consecutive wins in the series from 1956-65, until the Rams finally ended their skid with the wild 12-10 victory in Fort Collins on October 29, 1966. But the Cowboys avenged the Bounce Pass with a 13-10 win in Laramie in 1967 en route to the Sugar Bowl. Wyoming would extend its new winning streak to seven consecutive games during what turned out to be a bleak era for both sides of the rivalry.

After dismantling the Rams, 39-3, on October 4, 1969, the Wyoming program was rocked by the Black 14 incident less than two weeks later. Prior to the home game against Brigham Young University on October 18, head coach Lloyd Eaton dismissed the 14 black players from the team for requesting permission to wear black armbands to protest the policies of the Mormon Church, which did not allow blacks to enter the priesthood. The Cowboys, despite their success against Colorado State, suffered six consecutive losing seasons from 1970-75.

The Pokes' lone win in 1970, Eaton's final season, was a 16-6 triumph over the Rams in Fort Collins.

John Griffin, one of the 14 black players initially dismissed by Eaton, recalls many of the details of the Colorado State-Wyoming game in 1969 — including a costly wardrobe malfunction by Rams' star running back Lawrence McCutcheon — but he doesn't remember seeing the Bronze Boot.

"I remember the game because it was a cold day and the Rams came up to Laramie," Griffin said. "and Lawrence McCutcheon had on a pair of Playtex Gloves. I remember that vividly. He got loose across the middle, the ball was thrown to him, and with the cold and the Playtex cleaning gloves, the minute he caught it, it just squirted out of his hands. We avoided a score then and we went on and beat them that day.

"But I don't recall a trophy at all. With all the Border War conversation that comes up now every year, I don't recall that ever being talked about or there even being a trophy back then."

Perhaps it was just collecting dust on a shelf somewhere inside the Wyoming athletic department.

The Rams finished 7-3 in 1966 but were unable to get any bounce off the Bounce Pass season. Lude went 4-5-1, 2-8 and 4-6 over his final three seasons, finishing 1-7 against Wyoming during his seven seasons at Colorado State.

The Jerry Wampler era (1970-72) wasn't much better as the Rams went 8-25 overall and 0-3 in Border Wars. Then Sark Arslanian (1973-81) brought some much-needed swagger to the struggling Colorado State football program and shined a spotlight on the Border War.

"The times under coach Wampler were really hard. I mean, we were 1-10 in 1972," said former Colorado State quarterback Mark Driscoll (1971-75). "At the time when Sark came in, I remember he said it was going to take five years. And in five years he went from a team that was 1-10 to a team that was 9-4. He did a really good job. He knew what he was doing, how to build a team, he was a really good recruiter, he brought in good talent."

Colorado State pulled off a major upset of BYU in Provo, Utah, in Arslanian's second game. A 35-3 defeat in Laramie — the Rams' 17th loss in 18 meetings versus Wyoming — during a 5-6 finish in 1973 didn't sit well with the new head coach.

"Sark was a master at motivation and he invested heavily in getting us pumped up for the Wyoming game," said Jack Graham, who played quarterback for Arslanian in 1973-74 and later became Colorado State's athletic director. "He knew it meant a lot to our community, our school, and to each of us. It was bragging rights, and no one hesitated to brag if they won, on both sides.

"Charley Armey, our defensive coordinator, also contributed a lot to building the rivalry. He was an equally good motivator."

The Rams finally turned the series around with an 11-6 victory on a cold, soggy November Saturday in 1974.

"The weather was awful, the temperature was in the high 30's, and it was pouring down rain most of the game — the field was a mud bowl," Graham recalled. "Charley Armey chose to not wear a jacket, just a short-sleeve shirt, to show everyone that it wasn't that cold. I think he spent the next week in the hospital with pneumonia."

In 1975, Colorado State beat Wyoming 3-0 in another low-scoring tussle. It was the first time the Rams had defeated the Cowboys in back-to-back seasons since 1951-52 and their first victory in Laramie since 1955. Those milestones are what stick out most to the players of the era.

"I'd have to say it wasn't nearly what it is today," said Driscoll, who was the Colorado State director from 2003-06. "In 1975, even though the game was three-to-nothing and we didn't feel like we played real well, I remember saying, 'We beat Wyoming in Laramie.'

"It had been 20 years since it happened, so I remember it being a much bigger deal just by the fact that we beat them versus that we had the boot. At least in my recollection, the boot was not as big a deal in the early 70s."

Thurman "Fum" McGraw, Colorado State's first All-American, led the Aggies to upset wins over rivals Colorado, BYU and Wyoming in 1948 en route to the Raisin Bowl. The future College Football Hall of Fame inductee and Colorado State athletic director also experienced the agony of losing only one game in 1949 — 8-0 to the hated Cowboys in Fort Collins — which revitalize the football feud between the two schools.

During McGraw's playing days, the two small college towns had a lot in common. That's no longer the case with Fort Collins experiencing tremendous growth over the decades and Laramie staying mostly the same. Wyoming's dominance in the series in the 1950s and 1960s also took some of the luster off the series.

With Arslanian circling the game on the schedule, Colorado State extended its Border War winning streak to three games, the program's longest in the series since the 1940s, with a 13-3 win in front of a record crowd of 32,572 in Fort Collins in 1976.

"As Fort Collins grew, some of the charm of the series had gone away," said Tony Phifer, a longtime sports writer at the Fort Collins Coloradoan who is now a communications coordinator at Colorado State. "I remember talking to Fum one time and he said Laramie and Fort Collins were exactly the same size and kids knew each other and even dated each others' girls. When Fort Collins started to grow, and Laramie didn't, it sort of lost some of that. I think the rivalry always has meant a great deal to Wyoming, and there was a period where it didn't mean as much as CSU. . . .

"Sark really worked really hard to rekindle that."

The battle for the Bronze Boot really became heated as the Cowboys spoiled the Rams' run for a WAC title and a major bowl game with a 29-13 win in 1977. The infamous pre-game brawl broke out before Wyoming's 13-3 win in 1978 even kicked off.

"It was a big deal to win it back," Colorado State All-American defensive lineman Mike Bell (1975-78) said of the Bronze Boot.

"Being able to have that trophy handed to you was a real big deal, a prideful thing that you could hold on to for the rest of that year."

In the early 1980s, Jeff Romero decided to play at Colorado State as a walk-on defensive back for Leon Fuller, a defensive-minded head coach who played defensive back at Alabama for Paul "Bear" Bryant. After the Rams beat Wyoming 9-3 in a defensive slugfest in 1982, Romero said not much was made of the Bronze Boot during Colorado State's postgame celebration.

Wyoming seized possession of the trophy with wins in 1983-84. Colorado State reclaimed the boot with a 30-19 win in Laramie in 1985. Jeff Romero, who decided to go into ROTC and was on the sideline for the Rams' 20-15 win in 1986, decided to present the trophy to standout defensive back Jim King in the locker room at Hughes Stadium.

"I was on the field when Jimmy King had a four-interception performance and CSU beat Wyoming again," Romero said after King recorded more interceptions (four), tackles (three) against the Pokes.

"At that point I went over, grabbed the Bronze Boot off the stand and carried it across the field, holding it up. Then at the presentation in front of all the players I said, 'Jimmy, I've seen some exceptional performances, I've never seen a four-interception performance.' I handed him the boot, and said, 'This is for CSU.'"

In the previous Border War games, the ROTC units would bring the Bronze Boot to the winning locker room and give possession of the trophy to the team. Now players from the winning team run and grab the Bronze Boot on the sideline as soon as the game ends.

"Nobody ran to get the boot," Romero said. "The reason why I grabbed it and started to carry it was because they all knew me. I went into the locker room and they all knew me. I wasn't on the team, but I was in the ROTC and saw these guys all the time.

"I stood in front of the team and held it up on the bench. The whole team went crazy."

Wyoming returned the favor with a 20-15 win in 1987 in Laramie. Romero, who became the ROTC Cadet Commander at Colorado State, said the alma mater honored his dad as the donor of the boot during a ceremony at the 20-yard line during the 1988 game at Hughes Stadium.

"I know my father watches it intently," Romero said in 2017. "He's almost 80 years old now, born in 1937, so he'll be 80 this year. We care. We want to know, how are the Rams doing against the Cowboys?"

The 10th-ranked Cowboys pummeled Colorado State 48-14 in the 1988 meeting, which was part of a miserable 1-10 season for the Rams and brought about the end of the Fuller era. Colorado State hired former Ohio State coach Earle Bruce, a Woody Hayes disciple, to revive the floundering Rams. After a 56-35 loss in Laramie in 1989, Bruce notched a major Border War breakthrough with a 17-8 upset of 19th-ranked Wyoming on November 3, 1990. After the game the students tore down the goalposts at Hughes Stadium.

"I don't think I've ever been associated with a better win," an emotional Bruce, who had won or shared four Big Ten titles at Ohio State, said after the game. "I think this program had the farthest to go that I've ever gone to. It makes me so proud to be associated with those young men that have given so much hard work. I'm proud of our football team, and it was a team effort — one I'll remember for the rest of my life, I know that."

The hero of the 1990 game, Eric Tippeconnic, has no memory of what the postgame celebration was like with the Bronze Boot. Everything was kind of a blur after he intercepted a Tom Corontzos pass and returned it for a touchdown to seal a signature win for Bruce.

"I remember the Bronze Boot, but the funny part is I have no idea what happened after the game," Tippeconnic says with a laugh.

"From the moment I intercepted the pass and ran it in, it seemed to happen in slow motion. It's such a fast game, plays are over in just a couple seconds most of the time, and I just remember everything slowing down on that play. It was like I was reliving it while I was living it. I remember talking to myself while that play was going on, OK, you need to cut back, you need to head up field, secure the ball. I was actually talking to myself, it was that slow. Then it seemed like after I scored I immediately found my family in the stands and made eye contact with them. The rest of the game is a blur to me.

"I don't know if we ran over and got to the trophy or not, because the students started to spill onto the field, and I was right there with them. They were crawling on the goal post and I was in the crowd just celebrating with the students. Earle Bruce gave me the game ball, but I wasn't even in the locker room when he was talking to the team to accept it. I was still on the field celebrating with all the students."

Following the 1990 season, Wyoming coach Paul Roach retired after compiling a 35-15 overall record (3-1 vs. Colorado State) with three bowl appearances in four seasons. His top assistant, Joe Tiller, went 3-3 in the Border War, including wins over Bruce's Rams in 1991 and 1992.

Lubick, hired to replace the fired Bruce in 1993, and Tiller were on the opposite sideline for classic Border War finishes in 1994 (Colorado State's 35-24 win) and 1996 (Wyoming's 25-24 win).

"After the first game or two against Wyoming, I started to learn the significance of what it meant to the fans and the student body and the in-state players," said Lubick, who had a sparkling 11-4 record in Border Wars as Colorado State's head coach. "A lot of times you don't really know what your record is against this team or that team. But I did know what my record was against Wyoming, to be honest."

During the program's glory days under Lubick, the rivalry with Colorado became more of the focal point for many players and fans. But watching the Cowboys seize the boot from the sideline can bring the Border War back into focus quickly.

"It was one of those things you take for granted because we had it for so long and we'd been a dominant team," former Colorado State star quarterback Bradlee Van Pelt said of losing to Wyoming in 2003, which snapped the Rams' four-game winning streak in the series. "When you lose a game there and you kind of hand it back your senior year, it's really hard. It's the same thing as losing to (Colorado) my senior year. It was really kind of like, wow, for all the things we had, we're giving them back. How could it be my senior year we're giving back these trophies that we fought so hard to get used to having?"

Kevin McDougal, a standout running back for the Rams from 1996-99, explained the importance of the Bronze Boot at Colorado State this way:

"When that boot's not in your trophy case, you want it back in your hands as soon as possible. That's our trophy, it was a CSU student that wore that boot.

"When it's in their hands, it's a kick in the nuts."

The emotions that come with the annual gridiron battle for the Bronze Boot — from the ROTC detachments of each school running the trophy to the border for an exchange ahead of the game, to the postgame celebrations with the boot for the victor, to the sense of mourning for the losing side — make Captain Dan Romero proud to be an important part of the tradition every fall.

"I don't think he anticipated that it would grow to this fervor," Jeff Romero said. "The last conversation I had with him about it, he expressed elation that the boot grew to what it is. My father considers his children his legacy, but that's a nice addition to his life. He's completely overjoyed that it has grown to what it is."

The Other Rivals — Buffaloes, Cougars, Falcons

As passionate as both sides get about the Border War, there have been times when students from each school have saved their four-letter vitriol for another rival.

Older generations of Wyoming fans have vivid memories of the "F— you, BYU!" chants echoing from the student section at War Memorial Stadium, while recently Colorado State's students were the subject of a 2017 editorial in The Denver Post asking for an apology after they chanted "F— CU!" during the Rocky Mountain Showdown.

During the halcyon days of the Western Athletic Conference, Cowboy fans, especially those in the western part of the state, viewed Brigham Young University as the program's primary rival.

"If they can beat BYU, this whole season will go down as one of the greatest seasons of all time," Brady Poppinga, a defensive standout for the Cougars who grew up just north the Utah-Wyoming border in Evanston, Wyoming, told the Deseret News before the two programs renewed the rivalry in the 2016 Poinsettia Bowl. "And it would be one of their signature wins in the history of Wyoming football. It's a big deal for them."

The Colorado State rivalry with Colorado, which was dormant between the Rams' 15-14 win in 1958 and the Buffaloes' 31-3 win in 1983, has been a big deal in the Centennial State since the two programs began playing on an annual basis in 1995, with 17 of the last 20 meetings having been played in Denver.

"I think it's kind of a generational thing. People that are under the age of maybe 40 see CU as the big rival, no doubt, for CSU fans," said Kelly Lyell, the Rams beat writer for the Fort Collins Coloradoan, who grew up in Boulder. "Anybody older than the age of 40, it's clearly Wyoming, because much of their lifetime CU and CSU never even played each other."

Ask anyone who has played in or been associated with the Border War, and they will tell you how important the game is to their respective team, school, alumni and fan base. But in a series that began in 1899 (1900 according to Colorado State) with the two teams having played every year since 1946, there have been times where the rivalry lost its edge.

In the first 40 games, Wyoming won only five times, which was followed by the Cowboys winning 21 of the next 25. From 1993-2008, Colorado State won 12 of 16 games. Since 2009, Wyoming had won six of the last nine meetings through the 50th Bronze Boot game in 2017.

The University of Wyoming is the only four-year college in the state. Cowboy athletics — especially football — is the only show in town, so to speak. Fans who live in the eastern part of the state get a good sense of the Border War early and often. However, the further west you go in Wyoming, opinions of the Cowboys' biggest rivals differ — or used to.

BYU and Utah were longtime conference foes of Wyoming's going back to 1930. For many fans in western Wyoming, going to games at Utah in Salt Lake City, at BYU in Provo, and even at Utah State in Logan, gave them better opportunities to see the Cowboys play, rather than make the long drive to Laramie, where depending where you lived, can take anywhere from four to seven hours to drive one way.

Wyoming has played 83 and 78 games against Utah and BYU, respectively, in school history — second and third only to Colorado State. Fans in western Wyoming get a big dose of Utah media via television and radio, and over the years, as Utah and BYU became strong programs, fans were force-fed about all the success about those teams, and also how Wyoming, its athletic programs at the university and its fans were viewed as lesser-than by those who lived in Utah and were backers of the Utes and Cougars.

That wasn't the case from 1949-61 when the Cowboys won seven Mountain States Conference titles under Bowden Wyatt, Phil Dickens and Bob Devaney, or during the glory days under Lloyd Eaton when Wyoming won three consecutive WAC championships from 1966-68.

The program changed leading into the 1969 home game against BYU when Eaton kicked the 14 black players off the team for requesting to wear black armbands to protest Mormon Church policies they viewed as racist. Wyoming beat the Cougars, 40-7, but the program went into a downward spiral after the Black 14 incident, with only one winning season in the 1970s.

"That's why it was so tragic what happened to us," John Griffin, a member of the Black 14, said of Eaton's decision. "Had that team remained intact, we not only would have won the WAC in '66, '67 and '68, it would have been the same in '69, '70 and '71. There was nothing stopping us, and being as good as we were, we could have attracted even better athletes."

When BYU hired head coach LaVell Edwards in the early

1970s, and eventually became a national power for nearly 30 years, the rivalry with Wyoming grew bitter — at least among its fans — as the Cougars began to dominant the series.

Some of the Cowboys' most memorable wins and painful losses were against BYU.

"There was a time for Wyoming when BYU replaced CSU as their big rival," said Tony Phifer, a longtime Rams beat writer at the Coloradoan. "I think that was natural, too, because CSU was not good, and BYU and Wyoming were really good."

In 1981, Wyoming upset Jim McMahon and 13th-ranked BYU during a blizzard at War Memorial Stadium, which led to Edwards' memorable postgame quote: "I'd rather lose and live in Provo than win and live in Laramie."

The Cougars escaped with a 41-38 victory over Wyoming in Provo in 1984 en route to a 13-0 record and the program's national championship. Paul Roach's Cowboys beat BYU in 1987 and 1988 on the way to back-to-back WAC titles. The Cougars ripped the Pokes' hearts out with a 28-25 overtime win in the inaugural WAC championship game in 1996 in Las Vegas.

"Always good, hard-fought games. They always played hard," former BYU quarterback Ty Detmer, the 1990 Heisman Trophy winner who had five second-half turnovers in the 1988 meeting, told the Deseret News. "It was my first college experience playing in Laramie. It didn't go so well for me. I always looked forward to redeeming myself against Wyoming. They've always been a team that plays hard. They were always one of the better teams in the WAC at that time."

After the 2010 season, BYU and Utah left the Mountain West.

Utah joined Colorado (left the Big 12) as the Pac-10 expanded to become the Pac-12. BYU went independent in football. For both rising programs, the rivalry with Wyoming had already lost some of its competitive edge years before the realignment frenzy and the College Football Playoff era. Wyoming lost 11 of the last 12 games against Utah, and 14 of the last 16 to BYU, including a 24-21 gut-punch in the Poinsettia Bowl in San Diego.

"The fans wanted to send us home in our coffins," former BYU running back Hema Heimuli said after the Cougars' 31-28 win in Laramie on the way to the 1992 WAC championship. "They are worse than Utah fans. They cuss, throw beer bottles at you. You feel unsafe, like you need bodyguards. It's a nasty atmosphere up there."

When Wyoming dominated Colorado State from 1949-1973, the game was always important, just as the BYU series before the WAC imploded, but from the Cowboys' perspective there were other rivalries that matched the intensity.

James "Lefty" Cole is a Laramie native who lettered as a fullback for the Pokes from 1957-59. Cole said when he played, Wyoming's rivalry with Denver University was as big — or even bigger — than the one with Colorado State. Wyoming and Denver played each other in football 45 times between 1898 and 1960. From 1948 through 1960, the games in Denver were played on Thanksgiving. Cole recalls a memorable incident after the 1957 game in the Mile-High City.

"After the game we stayed in downtown Denver at the Brown Palace, and some players came in that night and had been partying," Cole said. "In those days, we had a lot of guys getting out of the service who were older, and Devaney didn't have much in the way of training rules.

"Some of the guys got smart with a security guard at the hotel. Somebody ended up decking a guy, and one security guard had his jacket sleeve torn off. He drew a pistol. Devaney then got involved and said if they were going to take any of his players to jail that he was going to go with them. Devaney, a couple of assistant coaches, and a couple of players spent the night in jail."

The Colorado State-Wyoming rivalry picked up with the introduction of the Bronze Boot traveling trophy. In 1968, the trophy was initiated by the ROTC detachments from both schools. The boot was originally worn in Vietnam by Dan Romero, a Colorado State ROTC instructor.

"The boot means more to the kids, where the Border War means more to us, unless there are kids that were passed over by CSU," said Wyoming senior associate athletics director Kevin McKinney, who has witnessed all 50 Bronze Boot games.

As the Bronze Boot portion of this rivalry enters its second 50 years, Wyoming has 26 victories, Colorado State has 24.

For Colorado State, the Rams have been the "little brother" to the University of Colorado since the two schools played their first football game against each other in 1893. In 89 games, the Buffaloes had won 65 times entering the 2018 season. There have been two ties in the series.

The two schools played each other pretty regularly from the late 1800s through 1958, but the series disappeared from the schedule for a quarter-century, and it wasn't until 1995 that the two programs began playing each other every year. To some associated with Colorado State, the annual game with Colorado has surpassed the rivalry with Wyoming. Former Colorado State quarterback Bradlee Van Pelt (2001-03) said as much, and helped the Rams beat the Buffaloes twice during that time.

"Bradlee Van Pelt made that statement, but that's never been in my heart," Gary Ozzello said. "Honestly, I think when people come here as student-athletes and have that perception they learn a hard lesson.

"Do we cherish the rivalry with Colorado? Absolutely, and a lot of that is the big brother syndrome."

From 1999-2002, Colorado State won three of four against Colorado, the most success it has had in the series going back to the 1930s.

"That to me was when Colorado transitioned into the spot for CSU fans as the top rival," Phifer said.

The Rams and their fans took out a lot of frustration on the 14th-ranked Buffs during the resounding 41-14 victory to open the 1999 season at the old Mile High Stadium in Denver. It was Colorado State's first win over Colorado since 1986. After the game, the Denver Police Department spoiled the fun, overacting to the green and gold party in the stands by spraying pepper spray and teargas on the crowd. Most of those fans in black and gold had left the stadium well before the end of regulation.

"It was certainly taking its place alongside the Wyoming game. It was no less a rivalry," said Steve Fairchild, who was Sonny Lubick's offensive coordinator from 1997-2000 before leaving for the NFL. "We started playing them on the neutral site in Denver. At one point I remember we sold it out at the old Mile High, and you felt like there were 35,000 in green and gold and 35,000 in CU colors. I believe that was the teargas game. Some of those games were impressive."

Colorado State went on to win a share of the Mountain West title in 1999, beating Wyoming 24-13 in Laramie along the way. The 2000 season began with the Rams' upsetting No. 23 Colorado, 28-24, for their first back-to-back wins over the Buffs since 1948-49. Colorado State won the MWC again, finishing 10-2, including a 37-13 romp over the Cowboys in the regular-season-finale.

"We always said we've got to beat Colorado twice in a row or two out of three to make this thing a rivalry," said Dan Hammer-schmidt, an assistant coach at Colorado State from 1996-2007 and from 2010-11, as well as a Wyoming assistant coach in 2009.

In 2001, Colorado State was ranked No. 24 before opening the campaign with a 41-14 loss to Colorado. Rams quarterback D.J. Busch threw three interceptions, including two that were returned for touchdowns, and was quickly supplanted as the starter by Van Pelt, who made his first start at Wyoming, leading the Rams to a 42-14 romp at War Memorial Stadium.

"I remember I was as nervous as can be," Van Pelt said of finally getting his opportunity to lead the Rams. "At that time, I started understanding the significance of the Wyoming game a little bit. I didn't fully appreciate the history because I was just so concerned with just trying to play. It wasn't like I was caught up in the history.

"My dad came in for the game. I didn't have a great game, but we won. That was always kind of my motto was: statistics are for losers. It was not about what I did, it was about what the team did and winning. That's the goal is to win. We won and that's what got me to them saying, he's the starter now."

Colorado State won 16 of the first 21 games Van Pelt started, including two Border Wars and an epic Rocky Mountain Showdown.

"Those were fun teams to cover because they kind of mimicked Bradlee and (wide receiver) David Anderson. They just had that swag to them, that swagger about them. They felt they could take on anybody and beat them anywhere," Mike Brohard said.

"That came directly from Bradlee and from David and the way they kind of approached the game. They didn't back down from anybody. As we all know, David was one of the best receivers of all time at CSU, and he wasn't the biggest guy on earth. Bradlee, at one point they wanted to make him a running back and he just flatly said no. Then they finally put him at quarterback, let him do what he could do, and then he became a better passer and was just exciting to watch. The team followed their mentality of how to play football and how they went about it."

Colorado State won its last three games of the 2001 season, capped with a victory over North Texas in the New Orleans Bowl, to finish 7-5 and set the table for another championship season. After a 35-29 win at Virginia in the 2002 opener, the Rams beat defending Big 12 champion and seventh-ranked Colorado 19-14 in front of a crowd of 75,531 at Invesco Field at Mile High.

"To me it felt like I was playing in the NFL already," said Van Pelt, who played for the Denver Broncos and Houston Texans after his ride with the Rams ended. "When you look up and see 76,000 people, when you're on TV nationally and you're ranked, and everyone's is talking about it, the fervor is high, and the intensity is there. I just remember being nervous at times, but I also remember kind of being exited to the point of thinking, this is why I wanted to be a quarterback, this is why I wanted to play quarterback, for these moments."

Van Pelt put a controversial exclamation point on the win by turning around and spiking the ball off the helmet of Colorado safety Roderick Sneed after scoring the decisive 23-yard touchdown with 6:20 remaining.

"That's really when it became a rivalry again for CSU was when Van Pelt did the famous spike off the helmet of (Sneed) in the end zone that game. That was kind of a big deal," Lyell said. "Earlier you had the teargas game. There were a couple years there where it became really contentious and became a great rivalry."

Van Pelt was unapologetic about "the spike" after the game and became public enemy No. 1 in Boulder. Sixteen years later, he said the infamous play was not intentional.

"It was all accident. It was the only time I've ever backpedaled into an end zone. I was taught very strictly in high school that when you score a touchdown, the ball goes to the referee. Literally, the first thing you do is the ball goes to the referee and you go congratulate with the team," Van Pelt said. "When I look at the play, and I still remember the play vividly, for some reason, I'm not really sure what caused me to start looking over my shoulder and then slowly starting backpedaling into it. But as (Sneed) reached out to kind of grab at my facemask it was a split-second natural reaction that happened. It happened at the goal line. You can imagine if it happened at the one-yard line, instead of this great play it would be a blunder. It's pretty interesting how close it was to being a blunder, but it ended up being a very significant and memorable play."

Colorado State went on to win the MWC again, sweeping the

Front Range with wins over Air Force and Wyoming along the way.

"The fun part about Bradlee was he gave us the quote afterwards, 'That's the worst No. 5 team in the country I've ever seen.'" Brohard said of the Rams' tone-setting win over Colorado. "That right then and there started the media policy changes. We weren't allowed to talk to players on the field directly after a game anymore. Now they have that cool-down period. And it wasn't too long after that when things really started changing and we weren't allowed in the locker room and we had to pull players out and ask for them and stuff."

Since Van Pelt's brash end zone celebration and harsh postgame comments about the Buffs, Colorado State is 4-11 against Colorado entering the 2018 matchup. The Rocky Mountain Showdown goes on hiatus again in 2021 and 2022, and the future of the rivalry is uncertain.

"Yes, I think that the Colorado game is viewed as a bigger and more important game than Wyoming . . . and frankly, at this point in time, I would agree," said former Rams quarterback Jack Graham, who was Colorado State's athletic director from 2011-14. "I think it's a tragedy that the CU-CSU game schedule will come to an end in a couple years. It has the potential to be one of the better rivalries in college football as CSU continues to improve, and with the new stadium venue at CSU, the games should be played on campus, not in Denver. And I think that the Wyoming rivalry will always be there, but Colorado has eclipsed that game in importance, in my opinion."

Mark Driscoll, another former Colorado State quarterback and athletic director, isn't comfortable with Colorado being considered the program's No. 1 rival by younger generations.

"I don't like it, honestly. I mean, it's good we're playing CU, it's fantastic," Driscoll said. "Because I'm old-school CSU, Wyoming is always the number one rival. I think graduates of the last, say 15 or 20 years, when the CU game has been regularly scheduled, will naturally think that the Buffs are the rival. In my mind, Wyoming and Air Force are both more of a rival than CU. Not that it's not nice to beat the Buffs, it is. Those three Front Range games matter to our fans. They're important."

The Air Force Academy is the other Colorado program that has been staking its claim as a significant rival to both Colorado State and Wyoming. Located just north of Colorado Springs, Air Force has been playing football against the Rams and Cowboys since 1957. It has played Colorado State every year since 1978, and Wyoming every year since 1980. Air Force leads the series over both schools — 28-25-3 against Wyoming and 34-21-1 over Colorado State.

"I can honestly say if CSU doesn't win the conference, I'm quite all right with it being Wyoming, but I certainly don't want it to be Air Force," said Derek Franz, who lettered as a kicker for Colorado State from 1997-98.

Two of the most memorable games, and comebacks, in the history of Colorado State and Wyoming football, came at Air Force's expense. During the 1988 season, the Cowboys entered the fourth quarter trailing 38-17 at Falcon Stadium. Wyoming scored 31 points in the fourth quarter, capped with a 27-yard field goal by Sean Fleming with four seconds left on the clock, to pull out a stunning 48-45 win for the largest comeback in school history. The Pokes also went on to win their second consecutive WAC crown.

"It really didn't sink in until after the game," said former

Wyoming quarterback Randy Welniak, who led the offense to scores on all five of its drives in the fourth quarter. "It was an amazing game that I will remember for the rest of my life."

The Air Force-Wyoming series has always been hard-fought, but the rivalry gained new heights in 2012. Air Force won in Laramie, 28-27, scoring a late touchdown for the victory. Wyoming head coach Dave Christensen unleashed a profanity-laced tirade at Troy Calhoun — which included calling his Air Force counterpart "Mr. Howdy F-ing Doody!" — as the two shook hands after the game. Christensen was frustrated with the loss, which dropped the Cowboys to 1-5. Christensen felt Air Force faked an injury late in the game to have more time to come up with the game-winning play. The verbal assault was caught on video and went viral on the Internet. Christensen was suspended for one game and fined $50,000 by athletic director Tom Burman. The next year, Wyoming went to Air Force and recorded its most lopsided victory in the series, 56-23.

"If you ask a lot of guys around here, they consider Air Force a bigger rival than CSU at times. It's crazy what the rivalry has turned into," said Wyoming wide receiver Dominic Rufran, who lettered for the Cowboys from 2011-14 and is from Colorado Springs.

During the 1996 season, Colorado State trailed Air Force 41-14 late in the third quarter before scoring the final 28 points of the game to pull off a 42-41 comeback for the ages. Rams quarterback Moses Moreno completed 31 of 48 passes for 358 yards and three touchdowns, including a 21-yard score to a diving Jeremy Calhoun with 45 seconds left. Air Force missed an extra point early in the game, and Colorado State placekicker Matt McDougal had to kick the decisive PAT after the Rams were penalized 15 yards for excessive celebrating.

"I'll never forget that game when we came back on Air Force when it was 41-14 and we are back and beat them in the fourth quarter," Fairchild said. "When Sonny took it over, the Wyoming game didn't lose its importance, but for whatever reason we started to bring CU back on the schedule and then we started to have some tremendous games with Air Force throughout his career in the '90s. It became like there were three rivalries all of a sudden, and if you could ever sweep them, which we did at one point, beating CU, Air Force and Wyoming all in one year was something hard to do."

Colorado State plays Colorado for the Centennial Cup and Air Force for the Ram-Falcon Trophy, but for most Rams fans the most significant regular-season hardware to collect is the Bronze Boot.

"There's no one in the world, other than the person that sculpted the Ram-Falcon trophy, that believes that Air Force-CSU is really a rivalry game. It's a game," Lyell said. "CSU-Utah State probably means more to most people. It doesn't mean anything special. Most of the Air Force players are not from Colorado. Sure, CSU likes to win it, but that was never a rival, never will be a rival, despite the fact that they have a trophy pretending it is. The real rivals have always been Wyoming, and then CU for the last 20 years because they've actually played each other. But when they stop playing again, that's going to disappear. I don't think it's going to be as big a deal and I don't think there seems to be any major push by CU to continue it beyond that. So, Wyoming will go back to being the main rivalry."

The Border War has stood the test of time with Colorado State and Wyoming belonging to the same conference since 1930. The rivalry remains a big one, thanks in large part to its longevity, close proximity between the schools and the fact both school are located

— as the name suggests — in bordering states. The head coaches and ROTC detachments from the schools meet every year at the border to exchange the game ball, which has added to the tradition and helped the Border War remain vibrant.

"I think now (the rivalry) has settled down to what it should be: A very important game on both teams' schedules, and it will be for as long as they're in the same conference," Phifer said.

Living on Both Sides of the Border

With the schools in close proximity to each other and relying heavily on recruiting players from the state of Colorado, there has been a fair share of crossover in terms of players and coaches in the Border War rivalry.

One of the more ironic instances was Mike McGraw, a linebacker who lettered for Wyoming from 1972-74. Kevin McKinney, who has worked in the athletic department since the early 1970s and does color commentary for Cowboys' football and men's basketball games, described McGraw as a "good player." Mike's brother, Dave, also played football at Wyoming but did not letter.

Mike's father, Thurman "Fum" McGraw, is one of the most recognized names in Colorado State sports history. He was the Rams' first consensus All-American (1948-49) as a defensive tackle.

Fum McGraw played for the NFL's Detroit Lions from 1950-54, where he was part of two championship teams and was a three-time all-pro selection. After his playing days, McGraw worked more than 40 years at his alma mater, including as an assistant football coach from 1955-57 and as the athletic director from 1976-86. McGraw is a member of the Colorado State University Hall of Fame, the state of Colorado Hall of Fame, the National Football Foundation Hall of Fame and the National Association of College Directors of Athletics Hall of Fame. The McGraw Athletic Center on the Colorado State campus is named in his honor.

"Just an incredible man of dignity and integrity and character," former Colorado State sports information director Gary Ozzello said of the legendary McGraw. "Of all the people I've ever met, he had the most unbelievable passion for CSU. I think it's ironic that both his sons and daughter went to Wyoming. Mike and Dave played at Wyoming. Dave also played for Lions. Fum's daughter, Debbie, was a cheerleader at Wyoming. "And here Fum is the ultimate Ram."

During his days as a student-athlete and fraternity member on campus, McGraw sang a song directed at regional rivals, known today as "Fum's Song," which includes a jab at the Border War rival:

I'll sing you a song of college days and tell you where to go.

Aggies, where your knowledge is, and Boulder to spend your dough.

C.C. for your sissy boys, and Utah for your times.

D.U. for your ministers, and drunkards School of Mines.

Don't send my boy to Wyoming U., a dying mother said.

Don't send him to old Brigham Young, I'd rather see him dead.

Just send him to our Aggies, it's better than Cornell.

Before I'd see him in Boulder, I'd see my son in hell.

It's unclear if Mrs. McGraw approved of her babies growing up to be Cowboys and putting on the brown and gold uniform, but Fum wasn't upset that his children played and cheered on the Pokes.

"I was not what you would describe today as a five-star guy," Mike McGraw said. "I was recruited by schools like Western State and UNC (Northern Colorado), back then it was Greeley Teachers College. Wyoming called me one day and said they would give me a full ride if I wanted to come up here and play football. I was a tight end at the time, and that's what they recruited me as. After I picked my jaw up off the floor, I said yes."

When asked if his father had an issue sending his two sons to Wyoming, Mike McGraw said: "Not at all. Dad loved Wyoming. He knew the coaches up here because he was a pro scout at the time."

Fum McGraw viewed the rivalry with Wyoming as important throughout his decades of service at Colorado State.

"During my time, Fum was at Colorado State, and I saw a big, grown man brought to tears, even before the game started, because it meant so much to him," said Kelly Stouffer, who lettered as a quarterback for the Rams from 1984-86 and now works for ESPN doing color commentary on college football broadcasts. "Fum was that way every year we played Wyoming. There was intensity, emotion and passion that didn't exist with any other game."

— — —

Marty English was an assistant coach at Wyoming from 2003-11 for two different coaches — Joe Glenn and Dave Christensen. He also was an assistant at Colorado State from 2012-17 for two coaches — Jim McElwain and Mike Bobo. English, a Colorado native with a stellar reputation for recruiting in that state, enters the 2018 season as the defensive coordinator for his alma mater, Northern Colorado.

While at Colorado State, English came under scrutiny from

Wyoming fans for his comments prior to the 2016 Border War game about Laramie and Fort Collins.

"I do know (Wyoming people) still come (to Fort Collins) for all their fun, their luxuries, all that kind of stuff," English said. "It's just not the same there. I know when that happens, it's like anything and you kind of look around at what everybody else has and you don't have and those kinds of things. There's some jealousy and stuff, and some harbor tough feelings. You have a different mindset when you have to live there (Wyoming) and when you have to live here (Fort Collins)."

English didn't say anything that was necessarily false, but that didn't sit well with Wyoming fans and the people who live in the state. He also described the Border War from the Pokes' perspective:

"This is their Super Bowl; this is their everything game," English said. "Well, it has to be as important to (CSU) as it is to them. And so, I still see it that way. My approach is still that way. . . .

"It's the boot. It's a rivalry game and it's the boot."

As the 2018 season begins, Colorado State assistant Bryan Applewhite has been with the Rams since 2015. Applewhite coached at Wyoming from 2003-08.

Oval Jaynes was a Wyoming assistant coach from 1978-80 and was Colorado State's athletic director from 1986-91.

Former Colorado State coach Leon Fuller (1982-88) was an assistant at Wyoming from 1975-76. He went 3-4 in Border Wars with the Rams and 0-2 with the Cowboys.

Steve Stanard was a Colorado State assistant from 2000-07 and Wyoming assistant from 2014-16.

Dan Hammerschmidt was a Colorado State assistant from 1996-2007 and again from 2010-11. One of those years away was spent at Wyoming in 2009. Hammerschmidt was part of Christensen's first staff that year, and the Cowboys rallied for a 17-16 victory over Steve Fairchild's Rams in Fort Collins to get Wyoming bowl eligible.

"No matter what side you are on, it was huge," Hammerschmidt said of competing for the Bronze Boot. "As a matter of fact, we always knew right where that sucker was on the sideline."

— — —

Most of the crossover in this rivalry involving players dealt with Colorado players coming up to play for Wyoming, including players from Fort Collins. A couple include linebacker Mark Brook and kicker Deric Yaussi. Brook lettered from 1992-94, and after his playing days returned to Fort Collins where he is a teacher and football coach at Rocky Mountain High.

"I was recruited by both Wyoming and Colorado State, but Wyoming, at the time, was a better fit for me," Brook said. "I was comfortable up there and it had nothing to do — good or bad — with Colorado State.

"At times it was a little interesting playing at Wyoming and being from Fort Collins. I had family members that were attending Colorado State and I was playing against their school. I never followed Wyoming much growing up, but once I got up to Laramie, it was home for me."

Brook said the 1994 game in Fort Collins, where Colorado

State rallied for a 35-24 victory and stormed the field, stands out to him as far as memorable games.

"We had some pretty intense games and it was a great, healthy rivalry, but there was nothing spiteful or anything like that," he said.

One of Brook's players, defensive end Teagan Liufau, will be a true freshman walk-on at Wyoming in 2018. Prior to that, the last Fort Collins player to play for the Cowboys was another of Brook's players, linebacker Kory Jones, who started his college career in junior college in Kansas and lettered for the Cowboys from 2011-12.

Yaussi lettered from 2002-06, led Wyoming in scoring in 2003-04 and is sixth in school history with 219 points.

One Fort Collins family got to see both sides of the Border War. Brothers Derek and Trenton Franz grew up in Fort Collins, and as Colorado State fans. Derek walked on as a kicker for the Rams and lettered from 1997-98. Trenton was a multi-sport star in high school, including being a swimmer despite his size as a lineman. Trenton signed with Wyoming. He was offered to walk-on at Colorado State, but didn't get a scholarship offer.

Trenton Franz lettered as an offensive lineman for Wyoming from 2001-04. He was a first-team All-Mountain West selection in 2004 and helped the Cowboys beat UCLA in the Las Vegas Bowl. Franz also was an academic All-American in 2004.

During the Sonny Lubick era at Colorado State, he and his staff didn't miss on many players in the recruiting process, but they did with Trenton Franz.

"It was pretty rough at the time. I knew Sonny quite well because my brother had just finished playing for him. One of my good friends, his mom was Sonny's secretary in the football office," Trenton Franz said. "But it also was a great motivator at the time. I packed up my bags and headed up to Laramie with a chip on my shoulder to prove what they missed out on over the course of my career."

However, there were some adjustments Trenton Franz had to make, and not just the move from high school to college football.

"Despite being 60 to 70 miles apart, the cultural differences between Fort Collins and Laramie are quite shocking," he said. "Coming from the Front Range to Laramie where it looked similar when I was there than it did in the 1950s was different. But I embraced the Cowboy culture and the rugged individual culture, which wasn't as prominent in Fort Collins, I would say."

At the time of Trenton Franz's recruitment, the Colorado State and Wyoming football programs were going in opposite directions. The Rams won or shared three Mountain West regular-season titles between 1999-2002 and played in five consecutive bowl games from 1999-2003. Wyoming won only nine games from 2000-03.

And, Wyoming defeated Colorado State only once when Trenton Franz was there — as a junior in 2003. Still, John Franz, Derek and Trenton's father, said the family "harbored some pretty tough feelings about Lubick" during Trenton's recruitment. Those feelings subsided over time. John said that Lubick told him in person he still "kicks himself" for not offering Trenton a scholarship.

Wyoming was the only Football Bowl Subdivision school to offer Trenton a scholarship, although he was heavily recruited by nearly all the Ivy League schools and also by Air Force, but he wasn't interested in a military career.

Being a longtime Colorado State fan, and then seeing one of his sons go to its biggest rival wasn't a big deal for John and the Franz family.

"We relished the fact he was going to play for Wyoming and try to beat Colorado State," John Franz said. "We were pissed off (at Colorado State) for not looking at him at all and asking him to walk on. Trenton wanted to play Division I. There was no animosity at all. We were glad to see him play and stick it to CSU."

But what about living in Fort Collins and having a son playing football for the rival team?

"There wasn't anything bad; most were quite understanding after explaining what happened and many were down on CSU that they missed on a local a kid that lived two and a half miles from the practice field," John said. "They couldn't understand why they didn't look at the kid. There was no, 'He's a traitor,' or stuff like that."

Derek Franz's experiences in the Border War were mixed. He was part of a 14-7 Colorado State win in Laramie in 1997, but he missed two field goals in that game. As a senior the next season, Wyoming won 27-19 in Fort Collins on the Rams' senior night — a game that is remembered by many as the "fog game" due to the haze that rolled in during the second half that made it difficult to see from one side of the field to the other. Derek missed a field goal in that game.

Derek Franz said he was "hurt" that Trenton didn't get a chance to go to Colorado State and experience the team success he had, but he was proud of that his brother got the opportunity at Wyoming.

However, there were some odd moments along the way. "I remember coming to Hughes Stadium when Wyoming played at

Hughes (Stadium) in 2000 when Trenton redshirted. It was weird sitting in the northwest corner of the stadium with Wyoming fans," Derek Franz said. "One of the really cool things was what both schools are about and their fan following. Being able to see it from both perspectives was really neat."

John Franz said he and his family support both schools' athletics departments and thinks both schools have a lot to offer in terms of academics. Derek Franz may not be the biggest Wyoming football fan, but his feelings are different now than they were as a player. However, that isn't the case with at least one of his former teammates.

"Back in 2011, I was coaching with Derrick Uhl, a tight end at Colorado State when I was there. He also was a graduate assistant for a couple of years at Colorado State," Derek Franz said. "From his perspective, it is all or nothing and he still can't understand how I can have anything positive to say about Wyoming."

— — —

There hasn't been a lot of Wyoming kids who played for Colorado State. Wyoming's small population isn't exactly a hot-bed for producing Division I football talent.

But there was a time during the Lubick era where a handful of Wyoming players headed south to Colorado State. It started with Mike Vomhof of Gillette, who lettered in 2001 and 2004. His brother, Bob, followed and lettered as a defensive end from 2004-07. Another Gillette product, offensive lineman Clint Oldenburg, lettered from

2004-06. Oldenburg was a second-team All-Mountain West selection as an offensive tackle. He was a fifth-round pick in the 2007 NFL draft by the New England Patriots and played for four different NFL teams during his five-year professional career.

Lubick and his staff also came into Cheyenne and signed brothers Ben and Dane Stratton from Cheyenne East High. Ben lettered as a defensive back from 2002-06. Dane lettered as an offensive lineman from 2005-08. The youngest Stratton brother, Alex, walked on for two years at Colorado State from 2008-09.

"You're put in a tough position because you're getting grief from all sides," Alex said. "One, that you went to Fort Collins and are playing for the Rams and not the Pokes, and from the other side from the Colorado folks knowing you are a Wyoming person. It's a tough position when most of the people you know are Cowboys fans and you're not, or on the other side."

Alex Stratton remembers going to a game in Laramie when Ben was playing. "The student section chanted 'Benedict Arnold' toward him," he said. "I remember some nastiness toward him from the Wyoming fans."

Ben Stratton's last couple of years in high school were when Wyoming football was at a low point. The Cowboys won just five games in coach Vic Koenning's three seasons (2000-02), and Colorado State was rolling. Alex Stratton said Wyoming didn't offer Ben a scholarship.

When Dane Stratton graduated, Joe Glenn offered him a scholarship. However, that was after Colorado State did the same. Alex said Wyoming was recruiting him in high school, and he thought there was some legitimate interest. But that went away, and later he found out by calling the Wyoming coaches himself that he was offered to walk on.

"When we would talk to a Ben or a Dane Stratton, they wanted nothing more than to beat Wyoming," said Mike Brohard, who covers the Rams for the Loveland Reporter-Herald. "It's the same way when you talk to Andrew Wingard (Wyoming's all-American safety from Arvada, Colorado) in the last couple years. They feel they didn't get that offer from their home state, so they want to hand it to them whenever they can.

"That's what makes the game a lot of fun is the Wyoming-Colorado kids that are involved."

— — —

Brian Hendricks was supposed to play football for Colorado State. His grandfather, Joe, was an offensive guard for the Rams in the 1950s. His father, Mike, was a fullback for the Rams from 1978-81. Brian was to be a third-generation Ram.

"As a child that was my dream," Brian said. "I remember going to games as a kid. I was always rooting for CSU. I wore CSU shirts, hats and jackets all the time."

Brian Hendricks didn't play for Colorado State, he played for Wyoming. English, a member of coach Glenn's staff, established a good relationship with Hendricks and his family, who live in Burlington, Colorado, a farming town with a population of about 4,200 in the eastern part of the state.

Wyoming was the first school to offer Hendricks a scholarship. Colorado State followed suit a few days after. Hendricks, who also was an outstanding high school wrestler with a 102-1 record, wanted to play linebacker. Colorado State wanted him to play running back. Hendricks went on his official visit to Wyoming first, and then to Colorado State the following week.

"I didn't see it as a possibility," Mike Hendricks said of his son choosing Wyoming over Colorado State. "By visiting Wyoming, I thought he would get there, see the difference between Laramie and Fort Collins, and he would run away (from Laramie)."

After returning from the Colorado State visit, the Hendricks family was back in Burlington. Mike and his wife, Nancy, were sitting in the living room when Brian had something to tell them. He said, "Dad, I really think I want to go to Wyoming," Mike Hendricks said. "I wasn't disappointed, I was just stunned, I guess. I had thoughts running through my head like, my dad is going to freak. All of the guys I played with are going to freak. But I just pushed that away and told Brian if that's what he wanted to do, I support him."

Joe Hendricks knew his grandson and English built a good relationship in the recruiting process, so when he found out Brian choose Wyoming: "I said, 'Okay, for five years I'm going to wear the brown and gold.'

"But it was a little hard to digest."

Brian Hendricks lettered for Wyoming from 2008-11 and earned All-Mountain West honors each of his last three years, including first team as a senior. He owns the Cowboys' single-game tackles record with 23 at Air Force in 2009.

The Pokes went 3-1 against Colorado State during Brian

Hendricks' stellar career, including three consecutive victories, two of which were in Fort Collins. The first, in 2009, gave the Cowboys their sixth win and bowl eligibility. Mike was on the sideline for that game.

"It's turmoil," he said "I went over and see a few of my friends on the other side of the stadium before the game and got no end of grief because I was wearing Brian's jersey and a Steamboat (Wyoming's logo) hat.

"I don't know how to describe it. You have loyalty that was built into your system for CSU, and you have your son playing for the other side. Blood is thicker than colors on uniforms. You go with your son.

"But over the five years Brian was at Wyoming, I had about 100 people come up to me and ask what the hell happened?"

The Next 50 — What will the future of the series look like in an ever-changing college football landscape?

The future of the Border War appears to be strong, but there is one thing that could derail it — another round of conference realignment.

When Missouri left the Big 12 Conference for the Southeastern Conference in 2012, its rivalry with Kansas (also called the Border War) left with it.

Colorado State was one of many schools that applied to join the Big 12 a couple of years ago, but the conference presidents decided not to expand.

"If there is another round of realignment and one of us was in a different league, that could cause pretty significant issues," Wyoming athletic director Tom Burman said. "You don't know how things will work out, when that happens or if it ever happens."

Many around the college football world don't wonder if there will be another round of conference realignment, but when it will occur. As the Power Five conferences continue to grow their resources, thanks in large part to television contract dollars, it makes it more difficult for the Group of Five leagues to compete — not that there wasn't already a major resource gap there. Some college football coaches believe the Power Five will consolidate to a Power Four at some point, which would make that resource and competitive balance gap even larger.

Former Colorado State athletic director Jack Graham said the NCAA needs to do something to create more parity in college football. He also believes the Rams need to find a way to get out of the Mountain West and into the Big 12.

"The lack of parity in college football is acute, and it's significantly about the money that comes to the schools that are in the Power Five conferences from media rights money," Graham said via email. "The NCAA is not doing its job. The Group of Five schools will be left behind, and the gap will grow larger if something isn't done to bring parity to the process."

Graham's suggestions for closing the gap between the haves and the have-nots include imposing a salary cap on the amount of money athletic departments can spend on all their programs, limiting football scholarships to 60 to spread the talent around, and expanding the College Football Playoff to eight teams, with a seat at the table reserved for a Group of Five representative.

"Lots can be done," Graham said. "If nothing is done, the Mountain West will be viewed more and more as a 'minor league' of college football, and the Wyoming game will be viewed with less interest."

Kelly Lyell, who covers Colorado State for the Fort Collins Coloradoan, doesn't forecast another sea change of realignment that includes the Rams being swept away from the Mountain West with an invitation from a Power Five conference.

"As much as Colorado State would like to move into another conference, I think it's unlikely," Lyell said. "Their best bet to actually become a legitimate major player in college football is for the entire Mountain West to elevate its profile. I just don't see them branching out on their own in some big conference and leaving Wyoming and Air Force and New Mexico behind. That's not to say it won't happen, but I don't see that as very likely."

For now, Colorado State and Wyoming are on solid ground for various reasons. One, both programs are having success on the field in recent years. Entering the 2018 season, Colorado State had played in five consecutive bowl games, something that had only happened one other time in its history (1999-2003).

Wyoming's recent success hasn't been as consistent, but progress has been made under head coach Craig Bohl. The Cowboys posted back-to-back winning seasons in 2016-17 for the first time since 1998-99. They played in consecutive bowl games during that time for the first time since 1987-88. And, if Wyoming reaches a bowl game in 2018, it will mark the first time in school history it would have done that in three consecutive years.

Although the Border War goes a long way to where both teams finish in the conference, and now, the Mountain Division of the Mountain West, both programs look to end long droughts of winning a conference championship. Colorado State's last title was in 2002. Wyoming's was in 1988 as a member of the Western Athletic Conference. However, the Cowboys won the Pacific Division of the WAC in 1996 and the Mountain Division of the Mountain West in 2016.

"I think Craig Bohl has done fantastic job, and coach (CSU coach Mike) Bobo is building a solid foundation," Gary Ozzello said. "I think it's critical for us to both have success for the long-term health of the Mountain West."

Two, both current head coaches know the importance of the

rivalry. Bobo and Bohl didn't grow up around the Border War and didn't become aware of it until they were hired prior to the 2015 and 2014 seasons, respectively. But they learned about the importance of the Colorado State-Wyoming game quickly.

"The Border War means a lot to our fans, and to Wyoming fans as well," Bobo said. "I know there's some hatred there between the two fan bases and the two teams. The majority of the people I've talked to told me Wyoming is our biggest rival, and former players going back 30 years ago said Wyoming."

Bobo added that he realized how big the Border War was less than two weeks on the job, and it had nothing to do with football.

"Wyoming and Colorado State were playing (men's) basketball. I was working late in the office and decided to go downstairs to the arena to check it out. The place was sold out and our students weren't back on campus yet," Bobo said. "I was like Holy cow! And, to see all the Wyoming fans at the game, I knew then this rivalry means something."

A lot of fans from Jackson to Cody to Cheyenne have a simple three-word message for Bohl when he travels around the state: Beat the Sheep!

"One of the very first groups of people I talked to when I got this job, and the group I pay attention to more than any other, is our former players," Bohl said. "To them, this is a big, big ball game and the one game each year they focus on. That makes it a big game for us. We recognize we are playing for more than what our football team is. This is a big game for our state."

Wyoming has no in-state rivals because it is the only four-year university in the vast, rural state. But Colorado State has a significant rivalry with Colorado. The two schools began playing football against each other in 1893 but have only played each other every year since 1995. The Rams have won only seven times since then and are 22-65-2 all-time against the Buffaloes.

"With Colorado it is different because we always had a chip on our shoulder because we didn't play them much," said former Colorado State quarterback Kelly Stouffer, a college football television analyst for ESPN who works many Mountain West games.

"Now that we do play them, we're kind of still treated like the little brother.

"With Wyoming, it is colleagues butting heads. You're in the same conference. You're fighting for the same thing, and you kind of always have."

When Brigham Young and Utah left the Mountain West after the 2010 season, two of Wyoming's bigger rivals in terms of history, and for fans who live in the western part of the state, went away. However, Wyoming trails the series 45-30-3 all-time against BYU, has lost eight straight games and 31 of the last 38. Utah is 51-31-1 against Wyoming and won 14 of the last 18 games. Isn't one aspect of a rivalry that each team beats the other somewhat frequently?

The future of the Rocky Mountain Showdown is also in question with no games between Colorado and Colorado State currently scheduled after the 2020 meeting.

"It's all disappearing here again after 2020," Lyell noted. "So, then Wyoming will undisputedly be the big rivalry again for CSU."

Mark Brook played high school football in Fort Collins and lettered as a linebacker at Wyoming from 1992-94. After his playing days, he returned to Rocky Mountain High, where he is a teacher and the head football coach.

"Being in Colorado, the publicity goes toward the CU-CSU game," Brook said. "If you look at (CSU) itself, and Wyoming being a conference game, even though CSU and CU have been playing a lot, you can't lose sight of how important the Wyoming-CSU game still is. My former players at CSU say Wyoming is still a big game."

Brook has two players on the Colorado State roster entering the 2018 season and will have one at Wyoming this fall.

Colorado State leads the series with Wyoming 58-46-5, but since the Bronze Boot was introduced in 1968, Wyoming holds a 26-24 edge. And in all of the games played between the two schools, the average score has roughly been 19-16 in favor of the Rams.

The two schools also have made financial commitments to football, including some impressive facility upgrades. Colorado State opened its $240 million on-campus stadium in 2017, and the first Border War game in that stadium will be played there in 2018. Wyoming debuted its $44 million High Altitude Performance Center earlier in 2018, which is located at the north end of War Memorial Stadium. It features state of the art enhancements to its weight room, training table, locker room, academic support and sports medicine facilities.

The Border War has withstood two world wars and 21 United States presidents. The two schools have had a combined 50 head coaches (32 for Wyoming, 18 for Colorado State). They've combined for 1,048 victories.

Times have changed since that first game in 1899, the one both schools can't agree upon in terms of the final outcome. There have been ebbs and flows in the rivalry, and it likely will take a dramatic shift in the national landscape for anything to change the future of the rivalry between the two programs and schools.

"It is like football between brothers," said Colorado State linebacker Deonte Clyburn, who lettered for the Rams from 2013-16 but didn't play in 2017 due to injury. "You don't want to lose. It is a game of who's tougher. It is always going to be a big rival. It is never going to go away. You get old-school, backyard football."

Burman grew up in Laramie, where the Bronze Boot resides in a special trophy case at the new football facility, courtesy of Wyoming's win in the snowy 2017 game.

"The two schools are less than 70 miles apart and recruit a lot of the same kids, and that makes a difference," Burman said. "When Wyoming goes into Colorado and gets an Andrew Wingard, who didn't have same opportunity at CSU, and he's up there laying the wood to those guys, that's what the rivalry is all about. That's what really moves the needle, at least from our side of it.

"From CSU's side of it, (Wyoming) is the school up the road they think they should be better than, and we think we should be better than them."

And the iconic traveling trophy that goes to the winner adds an extra layer of tradition.

Paul Roach was an assistant coach for Wyoming during its glory years from 1962-69. He also was the Cowboys' head coach from 1987-90 and the athletics director from 1986-96. As a coach and administrator, he was part of six of Wyoming's 15 bowl appearances and six conference championships.

Roach turns 91 on October 24 — three days before the 2018 Border War — and due to his advanced age wasn't confident enough to do a long, sit-down interview for this book. However, he may have summed up the Border War best for both schools. "It was never difficult to get up for the game, but it was awful difficult if you lost."

The Scores, Oh the Scores!

ALL-TIME BORDER WAR SCOREBOARD

Date	Location	Score
Nov. 30, 1899	Durkee Field | Fort Collins	Colorado St 12, Wyoming 0
Nov. 24, 1900	Durkee Field | Fort Collins	Colorado St 16, Wyoming 0
Nov. 14, 1903	Durkee Field | Fort Collins	Colorado St 17, Wyoming 0
Nov. 24, 1904	Prexy's Pasture | Laramie	Colorado St 6, Wyoming 6
Nov. 25, 1905	Durkee Field | Fort Collins	Colorado St 34, Wyoming 5
Nov. 14, 1908	Prexy's Pasture | Laramie	Colorado St 20, Wyoming 0
Oct. 16, 1909	Durkee Field | Fort Collins	Colorado St 32, Wyoming 3
Nov. 24, 1910	Prexy's Pasture | Laramie	Wyoming 10, Colorado St 0
Nov. 20, 1911	Durkee Field | Fort Collins	Wyoming 27, Colorado St 0
Nov. 28, 1912	Prexy's Pasture | Laramie	Colorado St 33, Wyoming 0
Nov. 27, 1913	Colorado Field | Fort Collins	Colorado St 61, Wyoming 0
Oct. 24, 1914	Prexy's Pasture | Laramie	Colorado St 48, Wyoming 10
Nov. 6, 1915	Prexy's Pasture | Laramie	Colorado St 48, Wyoming 0
Sept. 30, 1916	Colorado Field | Fort Collins	Colorado St 40, Wyoming 0
Oct. 6, 1917	Prexy's Pasture | Laramie	Wyoming 6, Colorado St 0
Sept. 27, 1919	Prexy's Pasture | Laramie	Colorado St 28, Wyoming 0

Date	Location	Score
Oct. 4, 1919	Colorado Field | Fort Collins	Colorado St 14, Wyoming 0
Oct. 2, 1920	Prexy's Pasture | Laramie	Colorado St 13, Wyoming 0
Oct. 16, 1920	Colorado Field | Fort Collins	Colorado St 42, Wyoming 0
Oct. 1, 1921	Colorado Field | Fort Collins	Colorado St 7, Wyoming 7
Oct. 14, 1922	Corbett Field | Laramie	Colorado St 60, Wyoming 0
Sept. 29, 1923	Colorado Field | Fort Collins	Colorado St 33, Wyoming 0
Nov. 26, 1925	Colorado Field | Fort Collins	Colorado St 40, Wyoming 0
Oct. 4, 1929	Colorado Field | Fort Collins	Colorado St 20, Wyoming 7
Nov. 8, 1930	Colorado Field | Fort Collins	Wyoming 20, Colorado St 7
Nov. 7, 1931	Corbett Field | Laramie	Colorado St 26, Wyoming 6
Nov. 24, 1932	Colorado Field | Fort Collins	Colorado St 23, Wyoming 0
Sept. 30, 1933	Corbett Field | Laramie	Colorado St 7, Wyoming 0
Nov. 3, 1934	Colorado Field | Fort Collins	Colorado St 16, Wyoming 0
Sept. 28, 1935	Corbett Field | Laramie	Colorado St 12, Wyoming 3
Oct. 17, 1936	Corbett Field | Laramie	Colorado St 0, Wyoming 0
Oct. 16, 1937	Colorado Field | Fort Collins	Wyoming 7, Colorado St 0
Oct. 1, 1938	Corbett Field | Laramie	Wyoming 0, Colorado St 0
Nov. 4, 1939	Colorado Field | Fort Collins	Colorado St 22, Wyoming 0
Oct. 5, 1940	Corbett Field | Laramie	Colorado St 0, Wyoming 0
Oct. 4, 1941	Colorado Field | Fort Collins	Colorado St 27, Wyoming 0

Date	Location	Score
Sept. 26, 1942	Corbett Field | Laramie	Colorado St 10, Wyoming 0
Oct. 5, 1946	Corbett Field | Laramie	Colorado St 7, Wyoming 0
Nov. 27, 1947	Colorado Field | Fort Collins	Colorado St 21, Wyoming 6
Oct. 16, 1948	Corbett Field | Laramie	Colorado St 21, Wyoming 20
Oct. 1, 1949	Colorado Field | Fort Collins	Wyoming 8, Colorado St 0
Oct. 7, 1950	War Mem. Stadium | Laramie	Wyoming 34, Colorado St 0
Oct. 13, 1951	Colorado Field | Fort Collins	Colorado St 14, Wyoming 7
Oct. 11, 1952	War Mem. Stadium | Laramie	Colorado St 14, Wyoming 0
Oct. 10, 1953	War Mem. Stadium | Laramie	Wyoming 21, Colorado St 14
Oct. 9, 1954	Colorado Field | Fort Collins	Wyoming 34, Colorado St 0
Oct. 8, 1955	War Mem. Stadium | Laramie	Colorado St 14, Wyoming 13
Oct. 6, 1956	Colorado Field | Fort Collins	Wyoming 20, Colorado St 12
Oct. 12, 1957	War Mem. Stadium | Laramie	Wyoming 27, Colorado St 13
Oct. 8, 1958	Colorado Field | Fort Collins	Wyoming 7, Colorado St 6
Oct. 10, 1959	War Mem. Stadium | Laramie	Wyoming 29, Colorado St 0
Oct. 15, 1960	Colorado Field | Fort Collins	Wyoming 40, Colorado St 8
Oct. 14, 1961	War Mem. Stadium | Laramie	Wyoming 18, Colorado St 7
Oct. 27, 1962	Colorado Field | Fort Collins	Wyoming 28, Colorado St 7
Oct. 12, 1963	War Mem. Stadium | Laramie	Wyoming 21, Colorado St 3
Sept. 19, 1964	War Mem. Stadium | Laramie	Wyoming 31, Colorado St 7

Date	Location	Score
Sept. 25, 1965	Colorado Field | Fort Collins	Wyoming 33, Colorado St 14
Oct. 29, 1966	Colorado Field | Fort Collins	Colorado St 12, Wyoming 10
Sept. 30, 1967	War Mem. Stadium | Laramie	Wyoming 13, Colorado St 10
Nov. 2, 1968	Hughes Stadium | Fort Collins	Wyoming 46, Colorado St 14
Oct. 4, 1969	War Mem. Stadium | Laramie	Wyoming 39, Colorado St 3
Oct. 10, 1970	Hughes Stadium | Fort Collins	Wyoming 16, Colorado St 6
Oct. 2, 1971	War Mem. Stadium | Laramie	Wyoming 17, Colorado St 6
Oct. 14, 1972	Hughes Stadium | Fort Collins	Wyoming 28, Colorado St 9
Oct. 20, 1973	War Mem. Stadium | Laramie	Wyoming 35, Colorado St 3
Nov. 2, 1974	Hughes Stadium | Fort Collins	Colorado St 11, Wyoming 6
Oct. 4, 1975	War Mem. Stadium | Laramie	Colorado St 3, Wyoming 0
Oct. 30, 1976	Hughes Stadium | Fort Collins	Colorado St 19, Wyoming 16
Oct. 29, 1977	War Mem. Stadium | Laramie	Wyoming 29, Colorado St 13
Oct. 28, 1978	Hughes Stadium | Fort Collins	Wyoming 13, Colorado St 3
Sept. 29, 1979	War Mem. Stadium | Laramie	Colorado St 20, Wyoming 16
Nov. 1, 1980	Hughes Stadium | Fort Collins	Colorado St 28, Wyoming 25
Oct. 31, 1981	War Mem. Stadium | Laramie	Wyoming 55, Colorado St 21
Sept. 11, 1982	Hughes Stadium | Fort Collins	Colorado St 9, Wyoming 3
Nov. 19, 1983	War Mem. Stadium | Laramie	Wyoming 42, Colorado St 17
Oct. 27, 1984	Hughes Stadium | Fort Collins	Wyoming 43, Colorado St 34

Date	Location	Score
Oct. 26, 1985	War Mem. Stadium | Laramie	Colorado St 30, Wyoming 19
Oct. 25, 1986	Hughes Stadium | Fort Collins	Colorado St 20, Wyoming 15
Oct. 31, 1987	War Mem. Stadium | Laramie	Wyoming 20, Colorado St 15
Oct. 29, 1988	Hughes Stadium | Fort Collins	Wyoming 48, Colorado St 14
Nov. 4, 1989	War Mem. Stadium | Laramie	Wyoming 56, Colorado St 35
Nov. 3, 1990	Hughes Stadium | Fort Collins	Colorado St 17, Wyoming 8
Oct. 26, 1991	War Mem. Stadium | Laramie	Wyoming 35, Colorado St 28
Oct. 24, 1992	Hughes Stadium | Fort Collins	Wyoming 31, Colorado St 14
Nov. 20, 1993	War Mem. Stadium | Laramie	Colorado St 41, Wyoming 21
Nov. 5, 1994	Hughes Stadium | Fort Collins	Colorado St 35, Wyoming 24
Oct. 28, 1995	War Mem. Stadium | Laramie	Colorado St 31, Wyoming 24
Nov. 16, 1996	Hughes Stadium | Fort Collins	Wyoming 25, Colorado St 24
Oct. 18, 1997	War Mem. Stadium | Laramie	Colorado St 14, Wyoming 7
Nov. 7, 1998	Hughes Stadium | Fort Collins	Wyoming 27, Colorado St 19
Oct. 23, 1999	War Mem. Stadium | Laramie	Colorado St 24, Wyoming 13
Nov. 16, 2000	Hughes Stadium | Fort Collins	Colorado St 37, Wyoming 13
Sept. 29, 2001	War Mem. Stadium | Laramie	Colorado St 42, Wyoming 14
Oct. 12, 2002	Hughes Stadium | Fort Collins	Colorado St 44, Wyoming 36
Nov. 1, 2003	War Mem. Stadium | Laramie	Wyoming 35, Colorado St 28
Oct. 22, 2004	Hughes Stadium | Fort Collins	Colorado St 30, Wyoming 7

Date	Location	Score
Oct. 22, 2005	Hughes Stadium | Fort Collins	Colorado St 39, Wyoming 31
Oct. 21, 2006	War Mem. Stadium | Laramie	Wyoming 24, Colorado St 0
Nov. 23, 2007	Hughes Stadium | Fort Collins	Colorado St 36, Wyoming 28
Nov. 22, 2008	War Mem. Stadium | Laramie	Colorado St 31, Wyoming 20
Nov. 27, 2009	Hughes Stadium | Fort Collins	Wyoming 17, Colorado St 16
Nov. 20, 2010	War Mem. Stadium | Laramie	Wyoming 44, Colorado St 0
Dec. 3, 2011	Hughes Stadium | Fort Collins	Wyoming 22, Colorado St 19
Nov. 3, 2012	War Mem. Stadium | Laramie	Wyoming 45, Colorado St 31
Oct. 19, 2013	War Mem. Stadium | Laramie	Colorado St 52, Wyoming 22
Oct. 25, 2014	Hughes Stadium | Fort Collins	Colorado St 45, Wyoming 31
Nov. 5, 2015	War Mem. Stadium | Laramie	Colorado St 26, Wyoming 7
Oct. 1, 2016	Hughes Stadium | Fort Collins	Wyoming 38, Colorado St 17
Nov. 4, 2017	War Mem. Stadium | Laramie	Wyoming 16, Colorado St 13

Colorado State

Coach

Earle Bruce: Inducted in 2002, 1989-92.

Players

Thurman "Fum" McGraw: Inducted in 1981, 1946-49.

Greg Myers: Inducted in 2012, 1992-95.

Wyoming

Coaches

Bob Devaney: Inducted in 1981, 1957-61.

Pat Dye: Inducted in 2005, 1980.

Bowden Wyatt: Inducted in 1997, 1947-52.

William H. "Lone Star" Dietz: Inducted in 2012, 1924-26.

Players

Eddie "Boom Boom" Talboom: Inducted in 2000, 1948-50.

Jay Novacek: Inducted in 2008, 1982-84.

Colorado State

1925: Kenny Hyde, QB (AP, third team)

1948: Thurman "Fum" McGraw, T (Consensus)

1949: Thurman "Fum" McGraw, T (Consensus)

1952: Harvey Achziger, T (International News Service, first team)

1955: Gary Glick, HB (AP, second team)

1975: Kevin McLain, LB (Sporting News/Time/Newspaper Enterprise Association, first team)

1977: Mike Bell, DL (AP, second team)

1978: Mike Bell, DL (Consensus first team)

1982: Jeff Harper, LB (AP, honorable mention)

1984: Keli McGregor, TE (UPI/AP, second team)

1986: Steve Bartalo, FB (UPI/AP, second team)

1994: Greg Myers, S (Football Writers/Sporting News/Scripps-Howard, first team)

1995: Greg Myers, S (Consensus first team);
Sean Moran, DE (second team);
Brady Smith, DE (second team)

1997: Anthony Cesario, OL (Sporting News, second team)

1998: Anthony Cesario, OL (AFCA, first team)

2002: Morgan Pears, OL (Sporting News, second team)

2003: Dexter Wynn, KR (CBS Sportsline, third team)

2004: Joel Dreessen, TE (SI.com/Pro Football Weekly, honorable
    mention)

2005: Kyle Bell, RB (SI.com, honorable mention);
    Jimmie Kaylor, P (SI.com/CBS Sportsline, honorable mention)

2013: Kapari Bibbs, RB (Walter Camp, second team; SI.com,
    honorable mention);

Shaquil Barrett, LB (SI.com, honorable mention)

2014: Rashard Higgins, WR (Consensus first team)

2015: Hayden Hunt, P (USA Today, second team; AP, third team)

2017: Michael Gallup, WR (Consensus first team)

Wyoming

1950: Eddie "Boom Boom" Talboom, TB (NEA/INS, first team; AP,
    second team);
    C.T. Hewgley, T (AP, second team);
    Dick Campbell, HB (AP, honorable mention);
    Tom Drost, End (AP, honorable mention);
    Dewey McConnell, End (AP, honorable mention);
    Selmer Pederson, S (AP, honorable mention);
    Doug Reeves, C (AP, honorable mention);
    Marlin Smith, G (AP, honorable mention);
    Marvin Strauch, T (AP honorable mention);
    Jerry Taylor, G (AP, honorable mention)

1951: Dewey McConnell, End (AP, first team);

Harry Geldien HB (UPI, honorable mention);

Doug Reeves C (UPI, honorable mention)

1953: Joe Mastrogiovanni, HB (UPI, honorable mention)

1956: Jim Crawford, HB (Look/NEA, first team;

Williamson Rating/INS, second team; AP/UPI/Football Digest, third team);

Buster Elder, End (AP, honorable mention);

Vince Guinta, C (AP, honorable mention);

John Watts, QB (AP, honorable mention);

Larry Zowada, HB (AP, honorable mention)

1959: Jerry Hill, RB (AP, honorable mention);

Len Kuczewski, G/LB (AP, honorable mention);

Jim Walden, QB (AP, honorable mention)

1960: Jerry Hill, RB (AFCA, honorable mention);

Marty Hamilton, End (Williamson Rating System, honorable mention);

Richard Williams, C (Williamson Rating System, honorable mention)

1961: Chuck Lamson, QB (UPI/NEA/Williamson Rating System, honorable mention)

1962: Glen Hopkins, T (AP, honorable mention);

Joe Vitale, G (AP, honorable mention)

1967: Jerry DePoyster, K (AP/Sporting News, first team);

Mike Dirks, DT (FWAA/NEA/Look Magazine, first team)

1969: Bob Jacobs, K (Sporting News/FWAA/Look Magazine, first team)

1976: Paul Nunu, LB (Football News, first team)

1977: Dennis Baker, OT (AP, first team)

1978: Ken Fantetti, LB (FWAA, first team)

1983: Jack Weil, P (Consensus first team)

1984: Jay Novacek, TE (Consensus first team)

1987: Galand Thaxton, LB (AP, third team)

1988: Pat Rabold, DT (AP, second team)

1990: Mitch Donahue, DE (FWAA/Sporting News/NFL Draft
       Report, first team)

1992: Ryan Yarbrough, WR (FWAA, first team)

1993: Ryan Yarbrough, WR (AP/FWAA, first team)

1995: Marcus Harris, WR (AFCA, first team);
       Brian Gragert, P (AFCA, second team)

1996: Marcus Harris, WR (Consensus first team); '
       Steve Scifres, OL (FWAA, first team);
       Cory Wedel, K (AFCA/Walter Camp, first team)

1997: Brian Lee, S (Consensus first team)

2001: J.D. Wallum, K (Football News, second team)

2005: Jovon Bouknight, WR (College Football News, honorable
       mention)

2006: John Wendling, S (College Sports Madness, third team)

2016: Chase Roullier, C (USA Today, second team)

BORDER WAR CONFERENCE CHAMPIONSHIPS

Colorado State

Year	Record	Conference
1915	7-0	Rocky Mountain Athletic Conference
1916	6-0-1	Rocky Mountain Athletic Conference
1919	7-1	Rocky Mountain Athletic Conference
1920	6-1-1	Rocky Mountain Athletic Conference
1925	9-1	Rocky Mountain Athletic Conference
1927	7-1	Rocky Mountain Athletic Conference
1933	5-1-1	Rocky Mountain Athletic Conference
1934	6-2-1	Rocky Mountain Athletic Conference
1955	8-2	Mountain States Conference
1994	10-2	Western Athletic Conference
1995	8-4	Western Athletic Conference
1997	11-2	Western Athletic Conference
1999	8-4	Mountain West Conference*
2000	10-2	Mountain West Conference
2002	10-4	Mountain West Conference

Wyoming

Year	Record	Conference
1949	9-1	Skyline Conference Champions
1950	10-0	Skyline Conference Champions
1956	10-0	Skyline Conference Champions
1958	8-3	Skyline Conference Champions
1959	9-1	Skyline Conference Champions
1960	8-2	Skyline Conference Champions*
1961	6-1-2	Skyline Conference Champions*
1966	10-1	Western Athletic Conference
1967	10-1	Western Athletic Conference
1968	7-3	Western Athletic Conference
1976	8-4	Western Athletic Conference*
1987	10-3	Western Athletic Conference
1988	11-2	Western Athletic Conference
1993	8-4	Western Athletic Conference*

(Note: Wyoming won the Pacific Division of the 16-team WAC in 1996 and the Mountain Division of the 12-team Mountain West Conference in 2016 but lost the conference championship game in each season)

*Tied for conference title

BORDER WAR BOWL PARTICIPATION

Colorado State

1949: Raisin Bowl: Occidental 21, Colorado State 20

1990: Freedom Bowl: Colorado State 32, Oregon 31

1994: Holiday Bowl: Michigan 24, Colorado State 14

1995: Holiday Bowl: Kansas State 54, Colorado State 21

1997: Holiday Bowl: Colorado State 35, Missouri 24

1999: Liberty Bowl: Southern Miss 23, Colorado State 17

2000: Liberty Bowl: Colorado State 22, Louisville 17

2001: New Orleans Bowl: Colorado State 45, North Texas 20

2002: Liberty Bowl: TCU 17, Colorado State 3

2003: San Francisco Bowl: Boston College 35, Colorado State 21

2005: Poinsettia Bowl: Navy 51, Colorado State 30

2008: New Mexico Bowl: Colorado State 40, Fresno State 35

2013: New Mexico Bowl: Colorado State 48, Washington State 45

2014: Las Vegas Bowl: Utah 45, Colorado State 10

2015: Arizona Bowl: Nevada 28, Colorado State 23

2016: Famous Idaho Potato Bowl: Idaho 61, Colorado State 50

2017: New Mexico Bowl: Marshall 31, Colorado State 28

Wyoming

1951: Gator Bowl: Wyoming 20, Washington & Lee 7

1956: Sun Bowl: Wyoming 21, Texas Tech 14

1958: Sun Bowl: Wyoming 14, Hardin-Simmons 6

1966: Sun Bowl: Wyoming 28, Florida State 20

1968: Sugar Bowl: LSU 20, Wyoming 13

1976: Fiesta Bowl: Oklahoma 41, Wyoming 7

1987: Holiday Bowl: Iowa 20, Wyoming 19

1988: Holiday Bowl: Oklahoma State 62, Wyoming 14

1990: Copper Bowl: California 17, Wyoming 15

1993: Copper Bowl: Kansas State 52, Wyoming 17

2004: Las Vegas Bowl: Wyoming 24, UCLA 21

2009: New Mexico Bowl: Wyoming 35, Fresno State 28 (2OT)

2011: New Mexico Bowl: Temple 37, Wyoming 15

2016: Poinsettia Bowl: Brigham Young 24, Wyoming 21

2017: Famous Idaho Potato Bowl: Wyoming 37, Cent. Michigan 14

BORDER WAR DRAFT PICKS

Colorado State

Year	Name, Round	Team
1960	Al Henderson, 1	Boston Patriots
	Ron Stehouwer, 1	Los Angeles Chargers
	Jeff Eifrid, 11	Washington Redskins
	Wayne Schneider, 1	Buffalo Bills
	Larry Womack, 2	Los Angeles Chargers
	Brady Key, 14	Pittsburgh Steelers
1961	Kay McFarland, 18	San Francisco 49ers
	Myron Pearson, 19	Houston Oilers
	Leo Reed, 20	St. Louis Cardinals
	Wayne Lee, 28	Denver Broncos
1964	Dick Evers, 15	Washington Redskins
1968	Jon Henderson, 3	Pittsburgh Steelers
	Oscar Reed, 7	Minnesota Vikings
	Al Lavan, 8	Philadelphia Eagles
	Mike Tomasini, 10	Atlanta Falcons
	Jim Oliver, 15	Detroit Lions
	Gene Layton, 17	Chicago Bears
1969	Bill Kishman, 5	Washington Redskins
	Terry Swarn, 6	San Diego Chargers
	Floyd Kerr, 16	Dallas Cowboys

1970	Earlie Thomas, 11	New York Jets
1971	Phil Webb, 11	Detroit Lions
1972	Lawrence McCutcheon, 3	Los Angeles Rams
	Jim White, 3	New England Patriots
1973	Perry Smith, 4	Oakland Raiders
	Gerald Caswell, 11	Dallas Cowboys
1974	Jimmie Kennedy, 9	Washington Redskins
	Greg Battie, 11	San Francisco 49ers
1975	Mark Mullaney, 1	Minnesota Vikings
	Al Simpson, 2	New York Jets
	Kim Jones, 7	Baltimore Colts
	Willie Miller, 12	Houston Oilers
	John Graham, 14	Miami Dolphins
	Pete Clark, 16	Dallas Cowboys
1976	Kevin McLain, 1	Los Angeles Rams
	Jerome Dove, 8	Oakland Raiders
	Melvin Washington, 11	Tampa Bay Bucs
	Dan O'Rourke, 13	Houston Oilers
	Gary Paulson, 13	Minnesota Vikings
	Mark Driscoll, 13	Dallas Cowboys
1977	Linden King, 3	San Diego Chargers
1978	Al Baker, 2	Detroit Lions
	Cliff Featherstone, 7	San Diego Chargers
	Mark Nichols, 8	Oakland Raiders
	Mike Deutsch, 9	Minnesota Vikings

1978	Ron Harris, 11	Minnesota Vikings
1979	Mike Bell, 1	Kansas City Chiefs
	Mark E. Bell, 4	Seattle Seahawks
	Mark R. Bell, 5	St. Louis Cardinals
	Bill Leer, 11	Atlanta Falcons
1980	Keith Lee, 5	Buffalo Bills
	Dupree Branch, 8	St. Louis Cardinals
1981	Alvin Lewis, 6	Denver Broncos
	Larry Jones, 10	Houston Oilers
1984	Kevin Call, 5	Indianapolis Colts
	Terry Nugget, 6	Cleveland Browns
1985	Keli McGregor, 4	Denver Broncos
	Harper LeBel, 12	Kansas City Chiefs
1986	Terry Unrein, 3	San Diego Chargers
1987	Kelly Stouffer, 1	St. Louis Cardinals
	Steve Bartalo, 6	Tampa Bay Bucs
	Steve DeLine, 7	San Francisco 49ers
1992	Selwyn Jones, 7	Cleveland Browns
1996	Brady Smith, 3	New Orleans Saints
	Sean Moran, 4	Buffalo Bills
	Greg Myers, 5	Cincinnati Bengals
	Raymond Jackson, 5	Buffalo Bills
1997	Calvin Branch, 6	Oakland Raiders
1998	Moses Moreno, 7	Chicago Bears

1999	Joey Porter, 3	Pittsburgh Steelers
	Anthony Cesario, 3	Jacksonville Jaguars
	Jason Craft, 5	Jacksonville Jaguars
	Darran Hall, 6	Tennessee Titans
2000	Clark Haggans, 5	Pittsburgh Steelers
	Erik Olson, 7	Jacksonville Jaguars
2001	John Howell, 4	Tampa Bay Bucs
	Rick Crowell, 6	Miami Dolphins
2004	Dexter Wynn, 6	Philadelphia Eagles
	Bradlee Van Pelt, 7	Denver Broncos
	Andre Sommersell, 7	Oakland Raiders
2005	Joel Dressesen, 6	New York Jets
2006	David Anderson, 7	Houston Texans
2007	Clint Oldenburg, 5	New England Patriots
2009	Gartrell Johnson, 4	San Diego Chargers
2010	Shelley Smith, 6	Houston Texans
2014	Weston Richburg, 2	New York Giants
2015	Ty Sambrailo, 2	Denver Broncos
	Garrett Grayson, 3	New Orleans Saints
2016	Rashard Higgins, 5	Cleveland Browns
	Cory James, 6	Oakland Raiders
2018	Michael Gallup, 3	Dallas Cowboys

Wyoming

Year	Name, Round	Team
1947	Hank Kolasinski, 23	Boston Yanks
	Jim Clayton, 21	Philadelphia Eagles
1950	Walker "Sonny" Jones, 28	Chicago Cardinals
1951	Jerry Taylor, 27	Chicago Bears
	Dick Campbell, 13	Washington Redskins
1952	Dewey McConnell, 3	Los Angeles Rams
	Harry Geldien, 19	Los Angeles Rams
1953	Chuck Spaulding, 12	Chicago Cardinals
1955	Frank Radella, 25	Washington Redskins
	George Galuska, 23	Detroit Lions
1956	Joe Mastrogiovanni, 17	Philadelphia Eagles
1957	Jim Crawford, 14	Pittsburgh Steelers
1959	Bob Sawyer, 11	New York Giants
	Dale Memmelaer, 21	Chicago Cardinals
1960	Jim Walden, 16	Cleveland Browns
1961	Jerry Hill, 3	Baltimore Colts
	2	Denver Broncos
	Chuck Lamson, 16	Oakland Raiders
	4	Minnesota Vikings
	Dick Schnell, 19	St. Louis Cardinals
1964	Will Radosevich, 22	New York Jets
	16	Philadelphia Eagles

1966	Darryl Alleman, 15	St. Louis Cardinals
	Jerry Durling, 6	Denver Broncos
	Jerry Marion, 10	Pittsburgh Steelers
	11	Boston Patriots
1967	Ron "Pedro" Billingsley, 1	San Diego Chargers
	Mike Davenport, 17	Pittsburgh Steelers
	Rick Egloff, 6	Oakland Raiders
	Don Klacking, 8	Philadelphia Eagles
1968	Jerry DePoyster, 2	Detroit Lions
	Jim Kiick, 5	Miami Dolphins
	Mike LaHood, 2	Los Angeles Rams
	Paul Toscano, 7	Houston Oilers
1969	Dave Hampton, 9	Green Bay Packers
	Gene Huey, 5	St. Louis Cardinals
1970	Larry Nels, 12	New York Giants
	Joe Williams, 12	Dallas Cowboys
	Vic Washington, 4	San Francisco 49ers
1971	Bob Jacobs, 7	Cleveland Browns
1972	Conrad Dobler, 5	St. Louis Cardinals
1973	Nick Bebout, 6	Atlanta Falcons
	Scott Freeman, 11	Detroit Lions
	Jerry Gadlin, 16	Oakland Raiders
1975	Archie Gray, 10	Pittsburgh Steelers
	Mike McGraw, 10	St. Louis Cardinals
1976	Lawrence Gaines, 1	Detroit Lions

1976	Aaron Kyle, 1	Dallas Cowboys
1978	Francis Chelsey, 6	New Orleans Saints
1979	Ken Fantetti, 2	Detroit Lions
1980	Danny Pittman, 4	New York Giants
1981	Guy Frazier, 4	Cincinnati Bengals
	Mandel Robinson, 12	Denver Broncos
1982	Gary Crum, 11	Miami Dolphins
	Jim Eliopulos, 3	Dallas Cowboys
1983	John Salley, 11	Atlanta Falcons
	James Williams, 10	New England Patriots
1984	Chris Kolodziejski, 2	Pittsburgh Steelers
1985	Jay Novacek, 6	St. Louis Cardinals
1986	Allyn Griffin, 8	Detroit Lions
1988	Jeff Knapton, 6	Los Angeles Raiders
1989	Eric Coleman, 2	New England Patriots
	Dave Edeen, 5	Phoenix Cardinals
	Pat Rabold, 9	Buffalo Bills
1990	Craig Schlichting, 8	Minnesota Vikings
1991	Mitch Donahue, 4	San Francisco 49ers
1992	Doug Rigby, 11	Kansas City Chiefs
1994	Ryan Yarbrough, 2	New York Jets
1995	John Burrough, 7	Atlanta Falcons
	Ryan Christopherson, 5	Jacksonville Jaguars
1996	Brian Gragert, 7	Denver Broncos

1997	Marcus Harris, 7	Detroit Lions
	Steve Scifres, 3	Dallas Cowboys
	Lee Vaughn, 6	Dallas Cowboys
2001	Patrick Chukwurah, 5	Minnesota Vikings
2004	Casey Bramlet, 7	Cincinnati Bengals
2006	Derrick Martin, 6	Baltimore Ravens
2007	John Wendling, 6	Buffalo Bills
2011	Chris Prosinski, 4	Jacksonville Jaguars
2014	Marqueston Huff, 4	Tennessee Titans
	Robert Herron, 6	Tampa Bay Bucs
2015	Mark Nzeocha, 7	Dallas Cowboys
2016	Brian Hill, 5	Atlanta Falcons
	Chase Roullier, 6	Washington Redskins
2017	Josh Allen, 1	Buffalo Bills

Sources

Interviews with Josh Allen, Michael "Mad Dog" Aanonsen, Charley Armey, Mike Bell, Mike Bobo, Craig Bohl, Casey Bramlet, Mike Brohard, Mark Brook, Tom Burman, Austyn Carta-Samuels, Dave Christensen, Deonte Clyburn, James "Lefty" Cole, Dana Dimel, Conrad Dobler, Mark Driscoll, Steve Fairchild, Ken Fantetti, Derek Franz, John Franz, Trenton Franz, Tom Frazier, Jack Gianola, Joe Glenn, John Griffin, Jack Graham, Ron Gullberg, Dan Hammerschmidt, Brian Hendricks, John Hendricks, Mike Hendricks, Sonny Lubick, Kelly Lyell, Kevin McDougal, Mike McGraw, Kevin McKinney, David Montgomery, Bruce Mowry, Gary Ozzello, Tony Phifer, J.J. Raterink, Paul Roach, Jeff Romero, Kelly Stouffer, Alex Stratton, Eric Tippeconnic, Paul Toscano, Drew Van Maanen, Bradlee Van Pelt, Jim Walden, Josh Wallwork.

Brohard, Mike. "Remembering Hughes: The Border War matters." *The Loveland Reporter-Herald,* September 28, 2016.

Call, Jeff. "Rivalry revisited: BYU-Wyoming rivalry filled with memorable games." *The Deseret News,* December 17, 2016.

Foster, Brandon. "Wyoming football mounts snowy comeback for 16-13 Border War win." *The Casper Star-Tribune*, November 4, 2017.

Hirn, John. *Aggies to Rams — The History of Football at Colorado State University.* Fort Collins, Colo.: John J. Hirn & ColoradoAggies.com.

McWhinnie, Ralph E. *Those Good Years at Wyoming U.* Casper, Wyoming: Prairie Publishing.

Meyers, Stephen. "Border War: CSU Rams forever Wyoming's No. 1 rival." *Fort Collins Coloradoan,* October 1, 2016.

Pope, Keegan. "Players, fans relive the greatest game ever played at Hughes Stadium." *Rocky Mountain Collegian,* November 6, 2015.

Stephens, Matt. "Fired from CSU, skydiving football coach 'bounced' back." *The Fort Collins Coloradoan,* December 28, 2015.

Thorburn, Ryan. *Black 14: The Rise, Fall and Rebirth of Wyoming Football.* Boulder, Colorado: Burning Daylight

Weakland, Steve. *A Million Cheers — 100 Years of Wyoming Cowboy Football.* Laramie, Wyoming: The University of Wyoming Football Centennial Committee.

Fort Collins Coloradoan, Wyoming Tribune-Eagle, Laramie Boomerang and *Laramie Republican* archives.

About the Authors

Robert Gagliardi and Ryan Thorburn first met as staffers at *The Branding Iron*, the University of Wyoming's student newspaper, in the early 1990s. Each author graduated from UW with a degree in journalism.

Gagliardi is a senior sports editor for *WyoSports.net* who has covered Wyoming football and basketball for 25 years. He has helped guide the *Wyoming Tribune-Eagle* to four consecutive "Grand Slams" — Associated Press Sports Editors top-10 recognition for daily, Sunday, special section and website. He also has helped the *Laramie Boomerang* win back-to-back Triple Crown honors from APSE in 2016-17.

Thorburn is currently a reporter for *The Register-Guard* (Eugene, Oregon) covering Oregon Ducks football. He was named the national beat writer of the year by the APSE for 2017. He previously covered the Denver Broncos and Colorado Buffaloes for *The Boulder Camera* and authored three Wyoming-based books — *The Black 14, Lost Cowboys* and *Cowboy Up.*